MARKET SIGNALS FROM
ONLINE BEHAVIOR

CONSUMER CORNER SERIES
UNCONVENTIONAL LESSONS FROM
CONSUMER BEHAVIOR

Why do consumers make the choices they do, and what can those choices teach us? The Consumer Corner series explores the subtle forces that shape consumer behavior, across topics that range from food, retail, health, vacations, and more. By spotlighting overlooked, counterintuitive, or nontraditional insights, the series challenges standard economic thinking and highlights the messy, human side of decision-making that sometimes occurs when humans engage in the marketplace. Drawing on behavioral science, lived experiences, and industry expertise, this series reveals what people can teach us as they make complex choices across the supply chain.

SERIES EDITOR

Nicole J. Olynk Widmar
Professor and Head of the Department Agricultural Economics
Purdue University

OTHER TITLES IN THIS SERIES

Decisions That Shape Supply Chains
Markets We Thought We Knew
Consumer Lessons From a Pandemic

MARKET SIGNALS FROM ONLINE BEHAVIOR

NICOLE J. OLYNK WIDMAR
MICHAEL L. SMITH
ERIN ROBINSON

Purdue University Press
West Lafayette, Indiana

978-1-62671-302-4 (paperback)
978-1-62671-303-1 (epdf)

Cover image: Debit card with laptop in cafe: Thomas Kirby/Unsplash.com

CONTENTS

INTRODUCTION

Market Signals From Online Behavior

You might recall from previous books in the *Consumer Corner* series: Consumers are fickle, they're demanding, they're (seemingly) uninformed—but they're also you. We want what we want, even if we don't know exactly what it is that we want, and we change our minds (a lot). For much of that seemingly unsavory behavior, we're unapologetic about it because we're spending our own money. And the customer is always right, right? Well, maybe. But it isn't that simple. Aside from how we behave, there's also lots of talk. Talk, talk, talk. Talk about products we bought and liked, bought and didn't like, didn't buy but wish we had, didn't buy and have no interest in but still feel compelled to share our opinions about. The list goes on. Bottom line is: We're a chatty bunch. And the cost of broadcasting our opinions—educated or not, factual or pretend—keeps going down. Now everyone with a Twitter account (okay, X, but really still Twitter) can share with the whole world. And they do.

Talk, talk, talk. We used to do it in person, face-to-face, or on the phone. We could do it one-on-one or in groups but getting together to do so came with costs. Then came the radio and television, where we could be talked at but not respond. Then the internet arrived, and suddenly we could be talked at from all directions—and finally, talk back. In so many forms. You can post on Twitter, share on Facebook, put a photo up on Instagram, make a longer video for YouTube or a shorter one for TikTok. And from the looks of the overwhelming quantities of media on just about everything, it appears that you're doing all of those things (twice). When did we start sharing pictures of food we didn't even make ourselves? And how are so many cats famous on TikTok? And why do I watch the cat videos? So many questions . . .

Allow me a quick trip down memory lane to where this all began. Our research team in Purdue University's Department of Agricultural Economics has gradually become a self-described academic think tank for human-oriented big data analytics in agriculture. Not the yield data, production data, or machine-collected field data. That's not where we're focused. We were focused on who did what, who bought what, and from where, and when. And of course, we wanted to know why. Sometimes it worked out and turned into full-blown multiyear research projects. Other times, it was whimsical fantasy. But our competencies today are the result of a journey that began when Nicole attended the Disney Data and Analytics Conferences (DDAC) in 2017 and 2018.

Nicole had long worked with survey data in the agricultural and food industries as part of her research program, but she sensed the opportunity to expand her capabilities to analyze and derive insights from other data sources, specifically online media data. While this field was progressing rapidly across a variety of industries, it remained largely underutilized within agriculture. In truth, most social and online media analytics happen at the brand or company level, rather than being framed in pragmatic research-oriented projects for public consumption. There are clear incentives for a company to study and understand perceptions of a name-brand product. But who was going to understand perceptions of pork or beef, broadly defined? Well, we would. Similarly, while a major concert might draw attention, what about agricultural and local fairs? We would do that, too. We want to know how public investments and societal investments in production or well-being are being talked about and received. The return on investment (ROI) is much more elusive when dealing with public goods, commodity products, and so-called basic or undifferentiated research topics in this online space. And that's precisely the gap we set out to fill.

Upon returning from DDAC in August 2017, Nicole enlisted her then-PhD student at Purdue University (now associate professor at

Oklahoma State University), Dr. Courtney Bir, in the challenge of collecting and analyzing online and social media data. Courtney was (rightfully) concerned, but never one to shy away from a challenge. With little more than a vague mission and no instruction manual, she got to work tackling how we would do this ourselves. The goal was to maintain control of the search and scraping process to ensure data quality to a level that would confer confidence for academic publication. What transpired between then and now was a multiyear flurry of a variety of new skill development sessions and a last-minute red-eye flight to Los Angeles so Courtney could train with Netbase (now Quid). Two agricultural economists navigating social media analytics was not the most predictable outcome, but it worked.

It took three years to produce publishable research at the caliber we had envisioned. In 2018, we presented our first sneak previews of this social media analytics vision at Purdue's Dawn or Doom conference. From there, the first of many public-facing research projects began to take shape. Each one has contributed something new to our team, whether a method, a dataset, or a new way of thinking. What follows are highlights of many of these projects, complete with lessons learned (mostly the hard way), as we continue exploring the intersection of digital chatter, consumer behavior, and agricultural economics.

1

A BRIEF HISTORY
OF THE INTERNET

Y ou may or may not easily recall that there was once a time when online news and social media were not common fixtures of life for the
average person. Not too long ago, most people rarely went "online"
or used a computer at all. Today, you no longer have to go online, because
you already are. All of the time. People now talk about going "offline," so-
lidifying "online" as our default state of being. Reflecting on this, it can be
shocking—especially for those born in the twenty-first century—to re-
alize that the world once operated entirely offline (and just fine), unbur-
dened (and unassisted) by the online world. Let's take a moment to revisit
the origins. The internet was only conceived as recently as the 1960s, first
demonstrated in the early 1970s, and did not become widely used for com-
merce until the 1990s—or perhaps even later.

In the context of recorded human history, the past two centuries have
brought dramatic revolutions in information exchange. The printing press
was foundational. In economic terms, it lowered the cost of information
exchange. Similarly, the telegraph, telephone, radio, and television accelerated that process, making information cheaper and faster to dissemi-
nate. All were revolutionary.

Following in the footsteps of these technologies, researchers in the United States and United Kingdom began experimenting in the 1960s with transferring information in packets over networks, rather than through circuits. This research, funded by the US Advanced Research Projects Agency (then ARPA, now DARPA¹), laid the foundation for the modern internet (Leiner et al. 1997). DARPA's influence on computing is widespread. The term "online" itself originated from an early ARPA project, oN-Line, which even predates ARPANET (DARPA 2025). The agency is also responsible for creating windows by which we interact with computer software, ranking results of file queries by relevance to the search terms, and even inventing the first computer mouse (DARPA 2025).

Initially, ARPANET linked researchers on the East and West Coasts of the United States, enabling shared computing resources. A successful public demonstration in 1972 caught the attention of the broader academic community (Leiner et al. 1997). By 1985, the National Science Foundation (NSF) was funding institutions to tap into ARPANET or similar networks—under the condition that the school receiving the grant make access available to anyone on its campus (Leiner et al. 1997). By this time, there were numerous networks of similar purpose across North America and Western Europe, and the NSF began to look for ways to make this infrastructure more useful to general audiences. Concurrently, the commercial world began to take an increasing interest in these technologies and became a conduit to make these networks more accessible and inclusive for broad communities of users (Leiner et al. 1997).

By 1995, the term "internet" had been formally adopted in the United States (Leiner et al. 1997). That same year, an estimated 14 percent of Americans had access to the internet, primarily through dial-up modems; meanwhile 42 percent of Americans reported having never heard of the internet (Pew Research Center 2014). At this time, anyone seeking access to the internet needed a computer. Phones were not capable of accessing the internet and tablets had not yet been invented (and it should go without saying that your household appliances, gaming consoles, motor vehicles, and airplanes did not access the internet either, and you most certainly weren't getting emails from your fridge to remind you to buy milk).

This time period between the 1990s and early 2000s saw transformative growth into what we now call the World Wide Web, or Web 1.0. This era enabled users to access linked documents and media for viewing with relative ease (Britannica 2025). Compared to today, the internet was limited to finding and retrieving information for the consumer to passively receive (Ledger 2023). There were no platforms for you to post your own photos, music, opinions, or wish a happy birthday to relatives, unless you made your own website.

By the mid-2000s, the internet saw another dramatic transformation. While static webpages for reading remained, a new interactive layer emerged: Web 2.0. This next wave allowed consumers to engage, comment, post, and connect through forums, blogs, consumer reviews, and of course, social media (Ledger 2023). Platforms like Myspace and Friendster were quickly replaced by platforms like Facebook, Twitter (now X), Pinterest, and many others.

The rise of these social networks runs in parallel with expanded access to the internet not only via enhanced infrastructure enabling access but also by the proliferation of internet-enabled devices. The widespread availability (and subsequent adoption) of smartphones in the late 2000s played a strong role in the evolution of Web 2.0 (Pew Research Center 2014). By 2023, 95 percent of the United States had internet access (Pew Research Center 2024a), and 83 percent of Americans reported using YouTube, with 68 percent using Facebook, making them the two leading social media platforms (Pew Research Center 2024b).

This digital ecosystem has fueled not just the growth of social media companies, but entire industries that successfully market *on*, *through*, and *with* them. It has also enabled a novel form of research in consumer and social science known as social listening. Social listening, a modern descendant of media monitoring practices that date back to the nineteenth century, involves capturing and analyzing unprompted mentions of topics across online platforms (Sonar Platform 2025).

The main merit of social listening lies in meeting the public where they are. In contrast to traditional surveys or interviews, social listening captures unsolicited opinions, posts, and mentions of topics that are unprompted by researchers and analysts. In doing so, social listening removes many of the biases that a researcher may inject into a study, even unwittingly, while designing a survey or experiment (Meltwater 2024). Given the large volume of social media activity, social listening offers researchers and industries large amounts of data, or what many call "Big Data" (Jung et al. 2022). These data can be leveraged to generate insights into sentiments, trends, complaints, market openings, emerging needs, and public response to real-world events in the market or policy changes. Of course, this data can be unruly. Researchers must navigate homonyms, slang, and evolving internet vernacular. Effectively storing, cleaning, and analyzing millions of posts is no small feat.

Still, as we seek to understand how consumers, or just people, make decisions, form preferences, and interact within food systems, retail markets, and broader economic systems, online and social media behavior offer a new frontier. Social media isn't the only data source being studied. Surveys, interviews, focus groups, news media, and even online search data all offer useful—and different—perspectives. Each data source comes with its own limitations and advantages. Online media data and social listening are not without their own limitations, and sometimes it isn't for the faint of heart (as the online world is an honest and sometimes inappropriate place). Online spaces aren't always polite, and they're not always clean. But they are real. There is much to be learned by studying what people say online when they know that everyone else can see them. We can learn from what they say, but also from what they don't say.

NOTE

1. Note that the organization originally known as ARPA switched to DARPA in the early 1970s, switched back to ARPA in the 1990s, and then a year later switched to DARPA again. This organization is not to be confused with the similarly named ARPA-E, which was launched in 2009 and is housed in the US Department of Energy.

WORKS CITED

Britannica. 2025. "World Wide Web." *britannica.com.* May 16. Accessed May 20, 2025. https://www.britannica.com/topic/World-Wide-Web.

DARPA. 2025. "Innovation Timeline." *darpa.mil/about/innovation-timeline.* Accessed 2025. https://www.darpa.mil/about/innovation-timeline.

Jung, Jinho, Nicole Olynk Widmar, Sangavi Subramani, and Yaohua Feng. 2022. "Online Media Attention Devoted to Flour and Flour-Related Food Safety in 2017 to 2020." *Journal of Food Protection* 73–84.

Ledger. 2023. "Web 1.0 Meaning." *ledger.com/academy.* November 21. Accessed May 20, 2025. https://www.ledger.com/academy/glossary/web-1-0.

Leiner, Barry M., Vinton G. Cerf, David D. Clark, Robert E. Kahn, Leonard Kleinrock, Daniel C. Lynch, Jon Postel, Larry G. Roberts, and Stephen Wolff. 1997. "A Brief History of the Internet." *internetsociety.org.* Accessed 2025. https://www.internetsociety.org/internet/history-internet/brief-history-internet/.

Meltwater. 2024. "The Ultimate Social Listening Guide—Never Miss a Social Mention." *meltwater.com/en.* October 15. Accessed May 20, 2025. https://www.meltwater.com/en/blog/social-media-listening-guide.

Pew Research Center. 2014. "Future of the Internet (Project) Part 1: How the Internet Has Woven Itself into American Life." *www.pewresearch.org/internet.* February 27. Accessed May 20, 2025. https://www.pewresearch.org/internet/2014/02/27/part-1-how-the-internet-has-woven-itself-into-american-life/#:~:text=In%201995%2C%20the%20Pew%20Research,U.S.%20adults%20with%20internet%20access.&text=Most%20were%20using%20slow%2C%20dial,with%20an%20expens.

Pew Research Center. 2024a. "Internet, Broadband Fact Sheet." *pewresearch.org/internet.* November 14. Accessed May 20, 2025. https://www.pewresearch.org/internet/fact-sheet/internet-broadband/.

Pew Research Center. 2024b. "Americans' Social Media Use." *pewresearch.org/internet.* January 31. Accessed May 20, 2025. https://www.pewresearch.org/internet/2024/01/31/americans-social-media-use/.

Sonar Platform. 2025. "Digital Media Monitoring: A Fascinating Brief History." *sonarplatform.com.* Accessed 2025. https://sonarplatform.com/digital-media-monitoring-a-brief-history/.

2

IS ONLINE MEDIA SENTIMENT A PERFORMANCE MEASURE YOU SHOULD CONSIDER?

BY NICOLE J. OLYNK WIDMAR AND COURTNEY BIR

A s the United States navigated the stages of reopening in 2020 from COVID-19 shutdowns—and countries around the world began returning to normalcy—one could not deny the central role that being (or *not being*) online played during those months. Internet access enabled people to work, attend school, stream entertainment, consult medical professionals via telemedicine, and perhaps most importantly, connect with one another. Family dinners via Zoom became common. Before quarantine, many toddlers had never encountered online conferencing software in their family lives.

Businesses, including those in food and agriculture, are online too. From websites and social media to mobile apps for in-field use and day-to-day internal communication, the World Wide Web plays a central role in operations. Even in agriculture, where rural infrastructure can limit connectivity, industry players increasingly depend on online tools and platforms.

There has been significant progress in understanding online presence through the combined efforts of computer science, marketing, analytics, and business management. This digital evolution has introduced, or strengthened, the potential for online and social media data analytics and related performance metrics. Sentiment analysis using social and online media derived data offers the potential to transform online qualitative data into a numeric score (Thelwall et al. 2010). Once sentiment, as a numeric value, can be assigned using a variety of techniques and algorithms to score language (commonly referenced as natural language processing), that numeric value can be compared to existing performance metrics such as stock prices (Schweidel and Moe 2014; Tirunillai and Tellis 2012). Past research suggests that sentiment is most useful when price-only prediction models lack accuracy (Nguyen et al. 2015).

Let's consider a relevant case study example: the iconic Walt Disney World Resort vacation destination in Orlando, FL. Our study, "Social Media Sentiment as an Additional Performance Measure? Examples from Iconic Theme Park Destinations" (published in the *Journal of Retailing and Consumer Services*, 2020), explored online media data related to Disney World and SeaWorld. We investigated how sentiment scores derived from social media posts related to traditional performance indicators like stock price and crowd scores (as a proxy for number of visitors). Disney World provided especially rich opportunities for analysis due to its sheer size and complexity, and at the time of study, it included twenty-five resort hotels, four main parks, two water parks, and a multitude of attractions and restaurants.

The nature of the multi-park and numerous resort complex of Walt Disney World allowed for more in-depth data analysis by differentiating resorts by Disney-defined classifications as well as delineating data by mention of specific parks (or attractions within that park). Social media mentions of individual parks were measured for the four ticketed parks (excluding waterparks) of Disney's Animal Kingdom®, Epcot®, Magic Kingdom®, and Hollywood Studios®. Resorts were grouped according to their classifications as outlined on the Walt Disney World Resort main website of deluxe, moderate, or value.... In total, in addition to the general Walt Disney World terms, seven sub-categories were developed consisting of the four parks named above and the three categories of resorts, grouped by the Disney-provided classifications. (*Consumer Corner*.2020.Article.01)

To discern if the sentiment, or the overall social and online media attitude (to be casual but still nearly correct) was related to more traditional performance indicators for Disney World and SeaWorld, we studied correlations between net sentiment and closing stock prices. The bottom line is that we found some evidence of a correlation between net social media sentiment related to Disney World and Disney's stock prices over the same time period. The accompanying figure illustrates monthly average stock prices alongside net social media sentiment. The most dramatic drop in sentiment aligned with online debate during the 2016 US election, when questions surfaced about whether Florida "deserved" Disney World. The second largest decline followed a tragic incident in which a young child was killed by an alligator on the banks of the resort's famous lagoon.

Pearson correlation coefficients revealed a statistically significant correlation of 0.3785 (p = 0.0515) between monthly net sentiment and Disney's average closing stock price. A parallel analysis of SeaWorld data did not find a significant relationship between stock prices and social media sentiment.

To conclude, past studies have found evidence of relationships between stock prices and online sentiment. Our study revealed mixed evidence: a modest correlation for Disney World, but not for SeaWorld. It is possible that sentiment and stock price are more closely linked for some companies, industries, or brands than others. Perhaps our selection of the iconic Walt Disney World as a case study was too much considering its extremely high familiarity with consumers. The sheer volume of mentions Disney receives may also have amplified our ability to detect a signal compared to a more localized or niche brand.

Perception matters. What people believe—and say—about your company online impacts your business and affects outcomes. Any number of hypotheses could explain what we and others observed, but one truth remains: Brands, industries, and even abstract ideas take on digital lives of

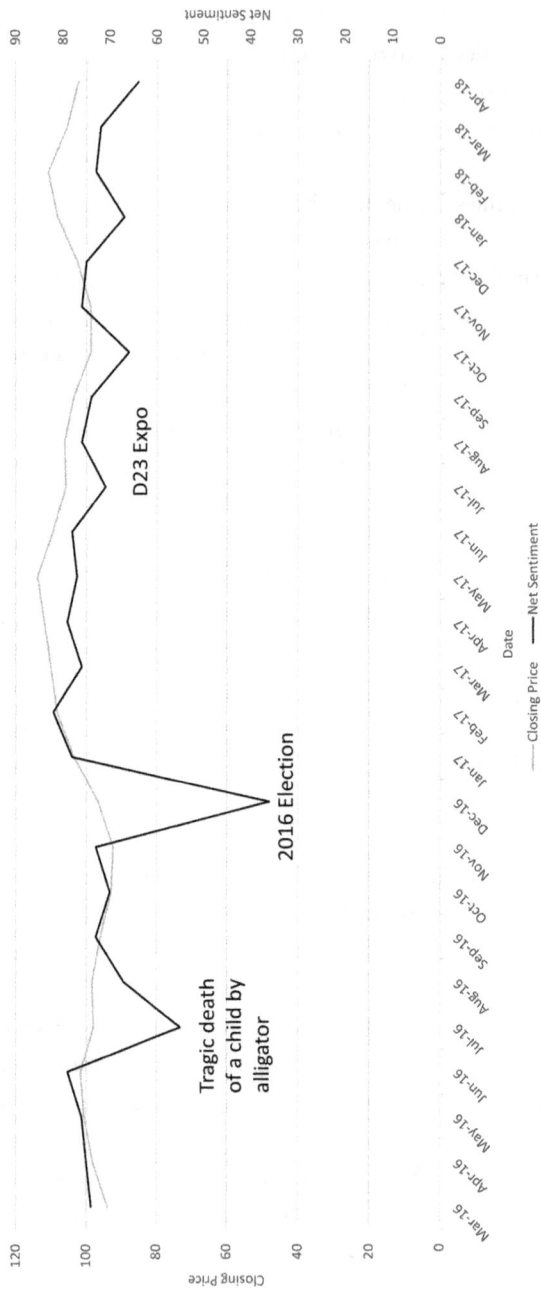

FIGURE 2.1. Stock Price and Net Sentiment at Parks Over Time

their own. While how best to use online sentiment data remains debatable, awareness of media impact is essential to our businesses and is especially real for agricultural and food industries. With so much of life now online, our digital reputations may matter more than ever.

WORKS CITED

Nguyen, Thien Hai, Kiyoaki Shirai, and Julien Velcin. 2015. "Sentiment Analysis on Social Media for Stock Movement Prediction." *Expert Systems with Applications* 42(24).

Schweidel, David, and Wendy Moe. 2014. "Listening In on Social Media: A Joint Model of Sentiment and Venue Format Choice." *Journal of Marketing Research* 387–402.

Thelwall, Mike, Kevan Buckley, and Georgios Paltoglou. 2010. "Sentiment in Twitter events." *Journal of the American Society for Information Science and Technology.*

Tirunillai, Seshardi, and Gerald Tellis. 2012. "Does Chatter Really Matter? Dynamics of User-Generated Content and Stock Performance." *Marketing Science* 198–215.

Widmar, Nicole. 2020. "Big Data" Provides Insights to Public Perceptions of USDA." *Agricultural and Applied Economics Association* vol. 35(01).

Widmar, Nicole Olynk, Courtney Bir, McKenna Clifford, and Natalya Slipchenko. 2020. "Social media sentiment as an additional performance measure? Examples from iconic theme park destinations." *Journal of Retailing and Consumer Services* 102–157.

Widmar, Nicole, Courtney Bir, John Lai, and Christopher Wolf. 2020. "Public Perceptions of Veterinarians from Social and Online Media Listening." *Veterinary Science.*

3

SOCIAL MEDIA'S POSITIVE PERCEPTION OF ANIMAL AGRICULTURE AT AGRICULTURAL FAIRS

BY NICOLE J. OLYNK WIDMAR AND COURTNEY BIR

For many people involved in agriculture, particularly those who participated in 4-H or FFA as children, the county or state fair likely holds a special place in their memories. There are notable differences across states in terms of timing and structure, but most county and state fairs share key attributes: youth livestock shows, commodity-focused fundraising efforts, and public education and outreach centered on agriculture. These elements remain reasonably consistent in concept, even if delivery varies geographically.

Some fairs have earned national recognition. The Minnesota State Fair, for example, is famous for its butter sculptures, which continue to receive media attention even during a canceled fair year (Martin 2020). And, of course, fair food is a category all its own—generating a following of extremely committed fans and frequent national media coverage. From deep-fried candy bars to iconic pork sandwiches and hamburgers topped with more hamburgers, the culinary culture of fairs invites debate, loyalty, and Food Network listicles (Khoury-Hanold 2025). Yet, at their core, these events are agricultural fairs—one of the last widely celebrated venues that consistently connect livestock agriculture with the general public.

In collaboration with Dr. Julie Mahoney, we studied how agricultural fairs are perceived by the public through the lens of social media. The result was a study titled "#GoingtotheFair: A Social Media Listening Analysis of Agricultural Fairs," in *Translational Animal Science* (Mahoney et al. 2020).

Similar to the methodology employed in the previous chapter, we used a prominent social media listening and analytics platform to quantify and analyze online media related to agricultural fairs over a twenty-seven-month period (July 1, 2017, to September 15, 2019). Our initial query gathered more than 2 million mentions (n = 2,091,350). We began with a search for online media that referenced agricultural fairs. We then dug into that dataset for references to fair food.

We filtered these references for more specific themes, including livestock mentions, fair food, and references to major agricultural species: dairy and beef cattle (n = 68,900), poultry (n = 39,600), and swine (n = 31,250). Online chatter around fairs followed a seasonal pattern, with Twitter emerging as the most popular domain for fair-related content. The overall tone of these posts using natural language processing capabilities (NLP), which calculated net sentiment by subtracting the percentage of negative posts from the percentage of positive ones. This score ranges from –100 percent to +100 percent.

Net sentiment overall was extremely positive, although mentions of zoonotic disease risk and other questions pertaining to animal agriculture did arise. Interestingly, politics at agricultural fairs was evident, as political candidates (more often in some states than others) use fairs as a means to address key stakeholders or interest groups. For the full analysis, see "#GoingtotheFair: A Social Media Listening Analysis of Agricultural Fairs" in *Translational Animal Science*, Volume 4, Issue 3 (Mahoney, Widmar, and Bir 2020).

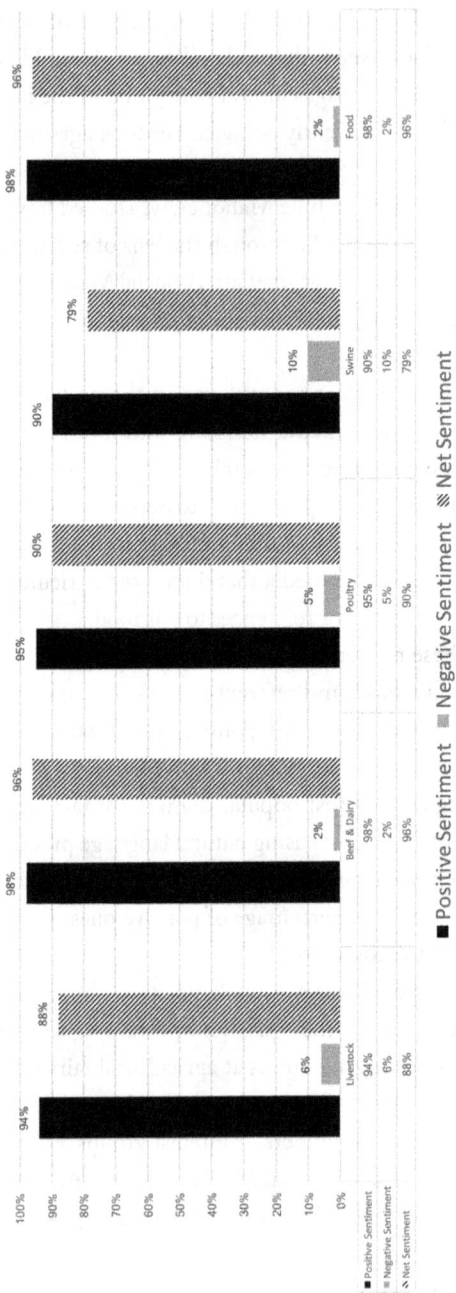

	Livestock	Beef & Dairy	Poultry	Swine	Food
Positive Sentiment	94%	98%	95%	90%	98%
Negative Sentiment	6%	2%	5%	10%	2%
Net Sentiment	88%	96%	90%	79%	96%

Positive Sentiment   Negative Sentiment   Net Sentiment

FIGURE 3.1. Net Sentiment of Online Media on Livestock at Agricultural Fairs

WORKS CITED

Khoury-Hanold, Layla. 2025. "The Best Fair Food in All 50 States." *foodnetwork .com/restaurants.* May 15. https://www.foodnetwork.com/restaurants/photos /50-best-fair-foods-by-state.

Mahoney, Julie A., Nicole J. Widmar, and Courtney L. Bir. 2020. "#Goingtothe-Fair: A Social Media Listening Analysis of Agricultural Fairs." *Translational Animal Science.*

Martin, Michael. 2020. "A Canceled State Fair Can't Stop Minnesota's Famed Butter Sculpture Artistry." *npr.org/2020.* August 30. https://www.npr.org /2020/08/30/907720075/a-canceled-state-fair-cant-stop-minnesota-s-famed -butter-sculpture-artistry.

Adapted from previous posting as *ConsumerCorner.2020.Letter.24* (https://agribusiness.purdue.edu/consumer_corner/social-medias-positive -perception-of-animal-agriculture-at-agricultural-fairs/)

4

THE SOCIAL LIFE OF FOOD IN A DIGITAL WORLD—A CASE OF THE INCREDIBLE EDIBLE EGG

BY YANGXUAN LIU AND JOHN LAI

S ocial and online media have hatched their way into nearly every aspect of our daily life, from direct marketing and health care to political campaigns. In 2008, only about one-quarter of Americans used social media. By 2019, that figure had risen to over 70 percent.[1] Growth continued in 2020, especially in light of when internet access became a vital tool for work, education, entertainment, health care, and perhaps most importantly, staying connected with others. Worldwide, there are nearly 4 billion total active social media users.[2]

As the web continues to connect people in the era of Web 2.0, users spend an average of 6 hours 43 minutes online daily,[2] generating enormous amounts of content every single day. During the pandemic, as people practiced social distancing, social and online media became essential for us to stay connected with our friends, family, and the outside world.

Traditionally, efforts to understand demand for food products relied heavily on past market performance and consumer survey data. While still useful, these traditional methods of measuring perception often rely on recall data. In contrast, the information social media users share online instantly creates opportunities to understand consumer experiences with the products that they use. This allows market-relevant data collection in real time with great efficiency, while surveys and focus groups ask users to recall information based on their past experiences. Employing this web-derived data for decision making within agri-food firms offers the opportunity for actionable insights tailored to individual businesses or products.

Researchers and data scientists alike have taken an interest in the digital expressions of consumer opinion. User-generated content (UGC) is now being used to understand consumer perceptions of various agricultural and food markets, including commoditized products like eggs. Food companies can take advantage of UGC on social media platforms and detect shifts in markets quicker than polling consumers through traditional methods such as surveys. As a widely consumed, affordable source of high-quality protein and key nutrients, eggs are a staple in many diets. However, evolving consumer perceptions around animal welfare increasingly influence demand for eggs produced using different production systems or technologies.

Research conducted by Widmar, Bir, Wolf, Lai, and Liu (2020), published in *Poultry Science*, employed social media listening techniques to understand consumer perceptions of egg-laying hen housing production systems in the United States (Widmar et al. 2020). The data collected for this analysis were intended to be inclusive of all social media referencing chicken eggs. Four housing systems for egg-laying hens were investigated: free-range, enriched colony, battery cage, and cage-free housing.

The research revealed that social media users discuss certain housing systems—particularly "free-range" and "cage-free"—far more frequently than others. These terms generated the most online hits among the four housing types examined.

Less online discussion surrounded "enriched cage," which could indicate that the public is either less familiar with or less engaged in conversations about enriched systems. However, this presents an opportunity: The enriched production system aligns with many consumer preferences related to animal welfare and sustainability, yet remains undercommunicated in online platforms.

These results, in conjunction with insights into net sentiment and online discussions, exemplify how social media listening may complement traditional methods to inform decisions in agribusiness marketing, food system design, production practices, and regulation.

So, if you are *egg-cited* by the *eggs-plosive* possibilities of social media data, we encourage you to learn more about the perceptions of social and online media users in the journal article on the subject of social perceptions of egg-laying hen housing (Widmar et al., 2020).

NOTES

1. Pew Research, "Demographics of Social Media Users and Adoption in the United States." Pew Research Center: Internet, Science & Tech. June 12, 2019. Accessed October 30, 2020. https://www.pewresearch.org/internet /fact-sheet/social-media/.

2. Data Reportal, "Digital 2020: Global Digital Overview." DataReportal— Global Digital Insights. January 30, 2020. Accessed October 30, 2020. https://datareportal.com/reports/digital-2020-global-digital-overview.

WORK CITED

Widmar, Nicole Olynk, Courtney Bir, Christopher Wolf, John Lai, and Yangxuan Liu. (2020). "#Eggs: Social and Online Media-Derived Perceptions of Egg-Laying Hen Housing." *Poultry Science*, 5697–5706.

Adapted from original posting as *ConsumerCorner.2020.Letter.28* (https://agribusiness.purdue.edu/consumer_corner/social-life-of-food-in -a-digital-world/)

5

ONLINE MEDIA SURVEILLANCE FOR THE PUBLIC (GREATER) GOOD?

BY NICOLE J. OLYNK WIDMAR AND COURTNEY BIR

O nline life has become a central part of everyday life for many of us, especially after the year that was 2020 (which somehow managed to feel like a decade). Social and online found themselves in the spotlight as many of us tried to work from home in a questionable state of attire (speaking only for myself). Grandparents Zoomed toddler playdates around the world, and we all reached some stage of "Zoombie" status. Realistically, we were already well on our way to cultivating and maintaining online lives that rivaled our in-person lives before the pandemic. Evidence included new movements to limit phone time, move away from social media, and tune in to human interactions after the pandemic. Yes, the pandemic accelerated a shift, but let's be honest: We were already heavily living online anyway.

During the lockdown period, *Consumer Corner* research was dominated by internet-based topics ranging from remote work and school to breakfast egg trends, Halloween, and how animal agriculture was being discussed at local fairs. You may or may not be horrified at the volume of work our collaborators generated while learning how to collect and use

FIGURE 5.1. Dawn or Doom: Social Listening Graphic

this type of data and apply the insights to agricultural and food research, marketing, and education.

The idea of using social listening and online media analytics at a public university for the public good has been mulled around in our research group from the start. Our first public-facing presentation on this topic was at the 2018 Dawn or Doom conference at Purdue University. That's when we debuted our first story about taking tools commonly used by big-name brands and applying them to commodity foods, such as eggs or milk (Gibson 2018).

At the Dawn or Doom conference, we provided sneak peeks into our then-ongoing data collection on public perceptions of holidays, Purdue

University, mosquitoes, and more. Shortly afterward, our focus on the perception of mosquitoes and the diseases they spread grew into a full-scale research project, which sought to quantify online media devoted to mosquitoes and determine what proportion of that was dedicated to the Zika virus (ZIKV) between 2016 and 2018.

ZIKV had broken into the US national news in 2016. We had previously conducted research on travel intentions of US residents, in the wake of ZIKV-related travel advisories, particularly concerning risks for pregnant women (Widmar, Dominick, Ruple et al. 2017). We also investigated the public perceptions toward using genetic modification to control disease-carrying mosquitoes and other vectors (Widmar, Dominick, Tyner et al. 20017). Clearly, at the time we collected data in 2016, people were concerned. We even found potential changes in behavior, such as avoiding travel to higher-risk travel destinations. But we wondered what the longer-term focus on ZIKV would be.

As it turns out, there wasn't one. Our findings were published in *Pathogens and Global Health* under the title "Public Perceptions of Threats from Mosquitoes in the U.S. Using Online Media Analytics" (Widmar et al. 2021). In the online media space, we discovered that while a significant share of mosquito-related online media in 2016 was devoted to ZIKV, that percentage declined rapidly by 2018. Although ZIKV remained a threat in some regions, public attention, as measured by online media volume, fell over time.

This decline has implications beyond Zika. As noted in our publication:

> Change or evolution of public interests, top words or things mentioned, or news coverage related to public health threats such as ZIKV, or the now critical COVID-19 pandemic, could potentially be assessed and responded to using understanding derived from online and social media data analytics. (Widmar et al. 2021)

While this project started before COVID-19, the idea of utilizing social and online media data and analytics to contribute to the understanding of public perceptions of public health threats had never been more relevant than in 2020.

WORKS CITED

Gibson, Kristen. 2018. "Purdue Professor Uses Social Media Analytics to Better Understand How People Perceive Food Products, Such as #Milk and #Eggs." *purdue.edu/dawnordoom*. September 18. https://www.purdue.edu/dawnordoom /news/News%202018/180919-Social-Media-Ag.html.

Widmar, Nicole J. Olynk, S. R. Dominick, Audrey Ruple, and Wallace E. Tyner. 2017. "The Influence of Health Concern on Travel Plans with Focus on the Zika Virus in 2016." *Preventative Medicine Reports* 162–170.

Widmar, Nicole J. Olynk, S. R. Dominick, Wallace E. Tyner, and Audrey Ruple. 2017. "When Is Genetic Modification Socially Acceptable? When Used to Advance Human Health Through Avenues Other Than Food." *Plos One.*

Widmar, Nicole J. Olynk, Courtney Bir, Evan Long, and Audrey Ruple. 2021. "Public Perceptions of Threats from Mosquitoes in the U.S. Using Online Media Analytics." *Pathogens and Global Health.*

Adapted from original posting as *ConsumerCorner.2020.Letter.32* (https://agribusiness.purdue.edu/consumer_corner/online-media -surveillance-for-the-public-greater-good/)

6

ONLINE MEDIA ANALYTICS IN AGRIBUSINESSES (OR LACK THEREOF)

BY JINHO JUNG, NICOLE J. OLYNK WIDMAR, COURTNEY BIR, JOHN LAI, W. SCOTT DOWNEY, AND AISSA GOOD

C ulnan et al. (2010) found that Fortune 500 companies use at least one of the most popular social media platforms to interact with customers, despite variations in platform usage by industry. In contrast, according to Brandwatch (2016a), agricultural industries are among the least developed in their use of social media. As of 2016, only 65 percent of agricultural firms had a social media presence, generating two million mentions annually about their brands.

In the first *Consumer Corner* letter of 2021, we explored new and online media as a way for agribusinesses to connect with customers. Yet not all agricultural firms present on social media are even active on the platforms where they have a presence. According to Brandwatch (2016b), only 1 percent of the 130,520 mentions directed to an agricultural brand over five months received a response. This lack of social media engagement may be attributed to the fact that agricultural firms largely belong to business-to-business (B2B) industries, where social media has been less developed or is perceived as less impactful. Regardless of the

reasoning, agriculture is still the least mature industry among B2B or-
ganizations, accounting for just 6 percent of total B2B brand mentions
(Brandwatch 2016b).

Social media use by firms is not limited to unilaterally conveying mes-
sages to the public or marketing strategies to consumers. Firms also monitor sentiment expressed in comments on blogs, review pages, or forums
via social media listening or social listening (used interchangeably) to
improve their products, services, or relationships with customers. Social
media listening has been showcased here in *Consumer Corner* over topics
such as eggs, Thanksgiving 2020, Halloween 2020, and even Disney World.

Companies sometimes react directly to campaigns put on by social activists. For example, Kraft Foods changed its ingredients in Kraft Mac-
aroni & Cheese after Food Babe and her army of supporters delivered a
petition with over 270,000 signatures and hijacked Kraft's Facebook page,
urging the company to remove the petroleum-based dyes Yellow No. 5 and
Yellow No. 6 (Veil et al. 2015). In 2003, Kraft Foods reduced the amount of
trans fat in Oreo cookies after carefully monitoring the public sentiment
on blogs (Terdiman 2006).

The scarcity and immaturity of social listening analytics in agricultural industries, especially when compared to other industries, is surpris-
ing. Agricultural companies at all stages across the vertical chain already
appreciate the value of data analytics (Pham and Stack 2018). For example,
seed input and machinery companies employ data analytics in their own
decision-making and help farmers make planting decisions, a practice
known as precision agriculture (Pham and Stack 2018).

However, an absence of B2B corporations from the social media space
does not necessarily mean there are no conversations surrounding the
brands. According to Brandwatch (2016b), social media platforms generate two million mentions about agricultural brands annually, and 59 percent of emotive language about agricultural firms is negative.

The relationship between actual agribusiness characteristics and management practices and the sentiment expressed in social media may
present a valuable opportunity. Agricultural firms can consider leverag-
ing public perception data to inform management decisions. In particular, social listening may help manage public relations issues before they

escalate—or, in the case of a crisis, provide a way to measure or monitor negative sentiment.

WORKS CITED

Brandwatch. 2016a. "Agriculture and Food Production Brands on Social Media." *brandwatch.com/blog.* https://www.brandwatch.com/blog/social-media-report -for-agriculture-brands/.

Brandwatch. 2016b. "B2B Industry Spotlight: Agriculture and Food Production." *Brandwatch.com/reports.* https://www.brandwatch.com/reports/b2b-industry -spotlight-agriculture-and-food-production/.

Culnan, M. J., P. J. McHugh, and J. I. Zubillaga. 2010. "How Large U.S. Compa-nies Can Use Twitter and Other Social Media to Gain Business Value." *MIS Quarterly Executive* 243–259.

Pham, X., and M. Stack. 2018. "How Data Analytics Is Transforming Agriculture." *Business Horizons* 125–133.

Terdiman, Daniel. 2006. "Why Companies Monitor blogs." *cnet.com/tech.* Jan-uary 3. https://www.cnet.com/tech/tech-industry/why-companies-monitor -blogs/.

Veil, Shari R., Jenna Reno, Rebecca Freihaut, and Jordan Oldham. 2015. "Online Activists vs. Kraft Foods: A Case of Social Media Hijacking." *Public Relations Review* 103–108.

Adapted from original posting as *ConsumerCorner.2021.Letter.4* (https://agribusiness.purdue.edu/consumer_corner/online-media-analytics -in-agribusinesses/)

7

DOCUMENTING POTENTIAL FOR ONLINE MEDIA ANALYTICS IN TOP SEED INDUSTRY AGRIBUSINESSES

BY JINHO JUNG, NICOLE J. OLYNK WIDMAR, COURTNEY BIR, JOHN LAI, W. SCOTT DOWNEY, AND AISSA GOOD

A nswering the call for online media analytics applied directly to agribusinesses, this analysis seeks to quantify the online media sentiment for five prominent agricultural corporations, all selected to have significant crop-related businesses. The agribusinesses analyzed and used to draw inferences, such as how imminently online sentiment reflects real-world incidents in the industry, were Bayer Crop Science (referred to as Bayer), DuPont, Land O'Lakes, Monsanto, and Syngenta. Although these businesses produce multiple products, this analysis focuses specifically on their seed production components.

The Quid (formerly Netbase) platform was used in this analysis, following the methodology presented previously here on *Consumer*

Corner. The search geography was limited to the United States, and only English-language posts were studied. Researchers developed datasets using targeted search terms (keywords), as well as exclusionary terms to eliminate irrelevant content. Search terms broadly encompassed agriculture, including words such as ranch, farm, agriculture, #ag, checkoff, and crop science. A total of 48 primary search terms initiated data collection.

Exclusionary terms helped ensure relevance. For example, FarmVille, while perhaps relevant to video gaming or sentiment around virtual farms, was not relevant to US agribusiness industries in US agriculture. Thus, the term FarmVille and all related references, in addition to State Farm insurance, bot farms, ranch-style homes, and ranch dressing, were removed from the parameters. A similar process was used to identify domains involving commentary that did not apply to the scope of this research. A total of 69 terms and 32 domains were identified and excluded by researchers.

Within this general search for agricultural industry content, five focused searches were conducted on top seed-related agribusinesses to allow for comparative analysis. Drawing from a list of top global agricultural companies by Castro (2015), the five companies—Monsanto, DuPont, Syngenta, Land O'Lakes, and Bayer—were selected for in-depth study. Along with Limagrain and KWS, these firms made up the top seven seed providers, accounting for nearly 90 percent of total global seed sales in the industry in 2017 (Zhang 2018). Among them, the top two seed companies, Monsanto (35 percent) and DuPont (26 percent) accounted for 61 percent of the worldwide proprietary seed market (Zhang 2018). Given the explicit focus on seed businesses, search terms for each company included key products and services, generated using each company's promotional materials.

The time period studied (December 1, 2015–February 15, 2018) was chosen to allow seasonality and annual factors to occur more than once, while also covering an important period of activity for the structure of agribusinesses in the United States. For example, the period chosen included announcements of three major mergers: (1) Dow Chemical and DuPont in 2015; (2) ChemChina and Syngenta in 2016; and (3) Bayer and Monsanto in 2016.

Data was collected and downloaded on March 4, 2018, with monthly timeline data (i.e., sentiment by month) downloaded on March 14, 2018. Given the fluidity of online and web-based datasets, all data was collected within ten days to maintain consistency.

Net sentiment presented throughout this analysis was calculated as the percentage of positive posts minus the percentage of negative posts. As such, it ranges from -100 percent (negative) to +100 percent (positive).

WHAT WE FOUND

Each business studied had different levels of involvement on social media during the study period. Monsanto, for example, lacked a central social media account but maintained branded accounts for subsidiary seed companies and brands. The other four companies engaged in social media strategies at both the conglomerate and subsidiary levels, although with limited activity. The absence of active posting on social media by B2B-focused corporations does not prevent related conversations from developing.

As mentioned, the study period encompassed several significant industry events. Three mergers were announced in 2015 and 2016. Dow Chemical and DuPont proposed merging in December 2015 (MacDonald 2019). Two months later, in February 2016, China National Chemical Corporation (also known as ChemChina) proposed purchasing Syngenta, a Switzerland agricultural chemical and seed firm, at $43 billion (MacDonald 2019). Finally, Bayer acquired Monsanto, confirmed in September 2016 after an initial offer of $62 billion earlier in May (MacDonald 2019; Gara 2016; de la Merced and Bray 2016; BBC 2016).

Substantial mention volumes were recorded monthly (see Figure 7.1).

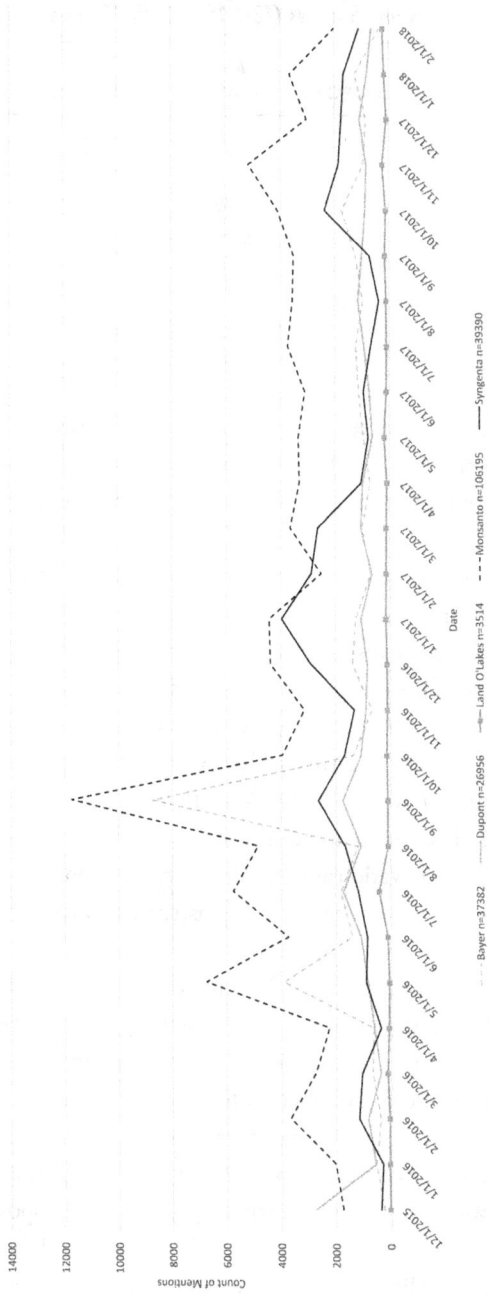

FIGURE 7.1. Monthly Mentions of Agribusiness Companies

Legend:
- Bayer n=37382
- Dupont n=26956
- Land O'Lakes n=3514
- Monsanto n=106195
- Syngenta n=39390

Y-axis: Count of Mentions (0, 2000, 4000, 6000, 8000, 10000, 12000, 14000)

X-axis: Date (12/1/2015, 1/1/2016, 2/1/2016, 3/1/2016, 4/1/2016, 5/1/2016, 6/1/2016, 7/1/2016, 8/1/2016, 9/1/2016, 10/1/2016, 11/1/2016, 12/1/2016, 1/1/2017, 2/1/2017, 3/1/2017, 4/1/2017, 5/1/2017, 6/1/2017, 7/1/2017, 8/1/2017, 9/1/2017, 10/1/2017, 11/1/2017, 12/1/2017, 1/1/2018, 2/1/2018)

TABLE 7.1. *Top Domains and Sources (12-1-15 to 2-15-18 Time Period)*

	BAYER	DUPONT	LAND O'LAKES	MONSANTO	SYNGENTA
Total Number of Mentions	60,750	40,545	4,480	152,339	48,210
News	69%	75%	59%	58%	40%
Twitter	18%	12%	21%	24%	53%
Blogs	11%	10%	13%	13%	6%
Forums	2%	2%	4%	4%	1%
Other		1%	2%	1%	0%

Table 7.1 presents sources for individual company searches. News was the most frequent source, with Twitter as the runner-up across all firms but Syngenta. Twitter was the top source for Syngenta with a small margin over News.

Net sentiment was positive for the five firms. Figure 7.2 reports positive, negative, and net sentiments.

Positive sentiments across the companies were driven by two attributes: the leading status of the companies and what they do for agricultural productivity. Negative sentiment drivers were varied and mostly related to mergers and their effects on farmers. However, the merger also showed up as a positive sentiment driver for DuPont. This may be because there are positive aspects of consolidation to the firms, such as economies of scale. Across companies, innovation and sustainability drove positive sentiment, while economic and environmental concerns, such as potash prices, drove negative sentiment.

Monthly net sentiment changed significantly over time (Figure 7.3). For example, Bayer's acquisition of Monsanto triggered an increased volume of chatter for the companies involved and substantial drops in net sentiment in May and September 2016. However, the approval of the Dow-DuPont merger in September 2017 received little social media attention. In contrast, ChemChina's proposal of acquiring Syngenta in February 2015 was widely discussed in early 2017, despite the proposal having occurred nearly a year earlier. These cases show that social media attention does not always align neatly with real-time corporate developments.

Positive, Negative, and Net Sentiments of Commercial Agribusinesses

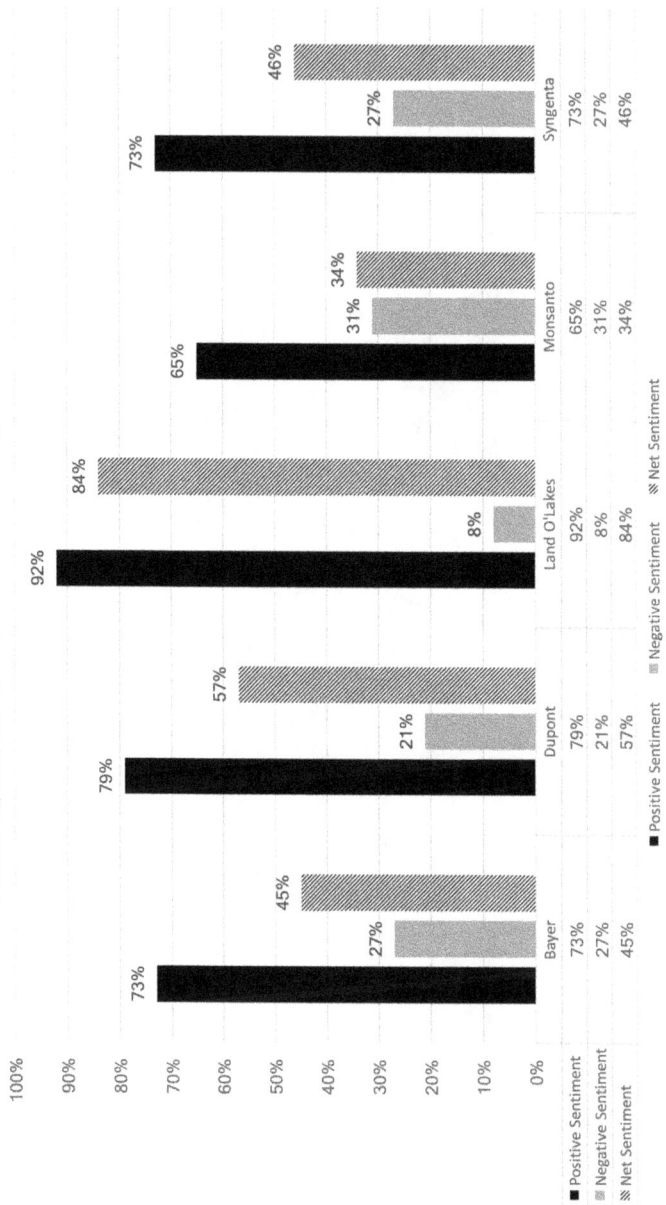

	Bayer	Dupont	Land O'Lakes	Monsanto	Syngenta
Positive Sentiment	73%	79%	92%	65%	73%
Negative Sentiment	27%	21%	8%	31%	27%
Net Sentiment	45%	57%	84%	34%	46%

■ Positive Sentiment   ▨ Negative Sentiment   ▧ Net Sentiment

FIGURE 7.2. Net Sentiment of Online Mentions of Agribusiness Companies

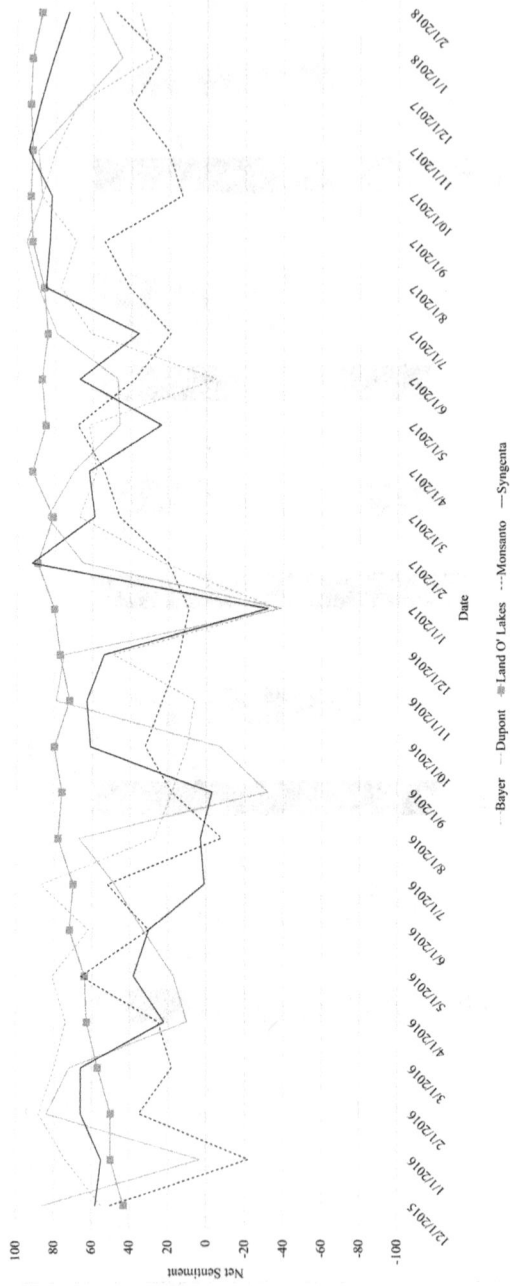

FIGURE 7.3. Monthly Net Sentiment of Agribusiness Companies

After the announcements of the mergers, net sentiment weakened due to public concerns over competition. Still, net sentiment generally remained positive. For example, net sentiment for DuPont dropped after the December 2015 announcement but stayed positive. Bayer and Monsanto also showed decreased net sentiment after Bayer proposed the acquisition of Monsanto in September 2016, while remaining positive. Syngenta's net sentiment fell both after the February 2016 proposal and the May 2017 approval, although net sentiment remained positive. Given that mergers and acquisitions have associated pros and cons, this neutralization of net sentiment around mergers suggests that social media reflects diverse views of various (opposing) parties.

SOMETIMES IT'S OUTSIDE OF YOUR CONTROL—BUT STILL IMPACTS YOU

Election Day 2016 had little to do with Disney World directly but mentions of Florida in election discussions—and debates over whether or not Florida deserved Mickey Mouse—impacted the overall sentiment toward Disney World because of it. Similarly, agribusinesses are not immune to adjacent media narratives.

On December 31, 2016, the *New York Times* published an article criticizing confidentiality agreements between corporations and universities. Though the article focused mostly on Syngenta and a disclosure of interviews with former Syngenta-affiliated scientists, other firms like Bayer, DuPont, and Monsanto were mentioned only briefly. But online media immediately reacted to this article with a New Year's Eve release date (when many were away from their offices).

Monitoring social media and reacting to negative spikes even during the holiday season may be pertinent for professional brand managers and communications professionals. Although the volume of chatter did not rise much, net sentiment fell sharply to -40. Given how net sentiment is calculated, the other potential aspect influencing this period is the relative lack of brand management from the corporations themselves, which would typically be positive postings taking place during business days.

Note that unlike the other four firms mentioned in the article, Land O'Lakes was not mentioned at all in the *New York Times* article and shows no downward change in net sentiment.

WORKS CITED

BBC. 2016. "Bayer Confirms $66bn Monsanto Takeover." *bbc.com/news/business.* September 14. https://www.bbc.com/news/business-37361556.

Castro, Arjylee Shing. 2015. "Top 7 Seed-Provider and Giant Companies in Agriculture Industry." *foundersguide.com.* July 10. https://foundersguide.com/top -agricultural-companies-in-the-world/.

de la Merced, Michael J, and Chad Bray. 2016. "Bayer Offers to Buy Monsanto for $62 Billion." *nytimes.com.* https://www.nytimes.com/2016/05/24/business /dealbook/bayer-offers-to-buy-monsanto-for-62-billion.html.

Gara, Antonio. 2016. "Bayer Offers to Buy Monsanto For $62 Billion." *forbes.com.* May 23. https://www.forbes.com/sites/antoinegara/2016/05/23/bayer-offers -to-buy-monsanto-for-62-billion/#7f80190fa461.

MacDonald, James M. 2019. "Mergers in Seeds and Agricultural Chemicals: What Happened?" *ers.usda.gov.* February 19. https://www.ers.usda.gov/amber-waves /2019/february/mergers-in-seeds-and-agricultural-chemicals-what-happened.

Zhang, Jason. 2018. "Top 20 Global Seed Companies in 2017." *accesstoseeds.org.* July. https://www.accesstoseeds.org/app/uploads/2018/07/Top20Global Seed.pdf.

———————

Adapted from original posting as *ConsumerCorner.2021.Article.2* (https://agribusiness.purdue.edu/consumer_corner/agribusiness -documenting-potential-for-online-media-analytics/)

8

MEDIA ABOUT YOU IS HAPPENING WITH OR WITHOUT YOU, AGRIBUSINESSES

BY JINHO JUNG, NICOLE J. OLYNK WIDMAR, COURTNEY BIR,
JOHN LAI, W. SCOTT DOWNEY, AND AISSA GOOD

Y ou didn't do anything wrong, but media about you is still about you—and it still matters. By 2021, we were all aware of the rampant mis- and disinformation online. But it doesn't have to be patently incorrect to be unflattering. For example, Disney World did not play a prominent (if any) role in the 2016 election, but it is in Florida; thus, media linked Mickey Mouse to politics, effectively tanking online sentiment about Disney World for a short period. Regardless, you want (need) to know what is being said by, about, or near you and your industry (and maybe even your competitors). On February 1, 2021, we released results about five top seed industry agribusinesses from our own online media analytics research. The core of those findings revolves around movement in volume (mentions) and net sentiment over time.

On December 31, 2016, the *New York Times* published an article discussing the relationship between scientists and agribusiness giants, including Syngenta (Hakim 2016). There are a few more abrupt drops in net sentiment without corresponding increases in volume, namely Monsanto in

February and August 2016; Syngenta in September 2016; DuPont in September 2016; and Bayer in June 2017 (see figures 8.1 and 8.2). These drops are not related to the mergers or the *New York Times* article, but rather, they are reflective of other media activities. Briefly scanning chronologically:

1. Monsanto paid an $80 million penalty for violating accounting principles and improper rebate accounting in February 2016 (Orpurt 2016; SEC 2016).

2. Monsanto was also mentioned in several social media posts in August 2016 for dicamba-related crop damage in Missouri and Arkansas (Bunge 2014; Cassidy 2016; Charles 2016; Philpott 2016).

3. In September 2016, the US Environmental Protection Agency (EPA) announced Syngenta violated the Federal Insecticide, Fungicide, and Rodenticide Act (FIFRA) and EPA's Pesticide Container and Containment Rule (PCCR). Syngenta agreed to pay $1.2 million to resolve its alleged violation (Campbell and Burchi 2016; Davies 2016).

4. DuPont retirees were worried that their pension plan would be changed as a result of the merger. One of them started running a Facebook group called DuPont Pensioners with around 8.1 thousand members (Tullo 2016).

5. In June 2017, Bayer's stock shares plummeted after a profit warning for Bayer over its performance in agrochemical and over-the-counter medicines was announced (Megaw 2017; Rehman 2017).

These documented relationships between real-world events and changes in social media volume and net sentiment suggest that agribusinesses and related agricultural industries could potentially benefit from conducting social listening analysis to aid in managing their public relations. When social media sentiment turns downward, it can be helpful for the impacted industries or firms to know precisely what is driving that change. It is crucial for firms to understand incidents or media narratives to recover brand perception and defuse situations appropriately and in a timely manner. Considering how imminently social sentiment reflects reality, it is highly recommended that agricultural companies consider active social listening as one of their tools to maintain brand image.

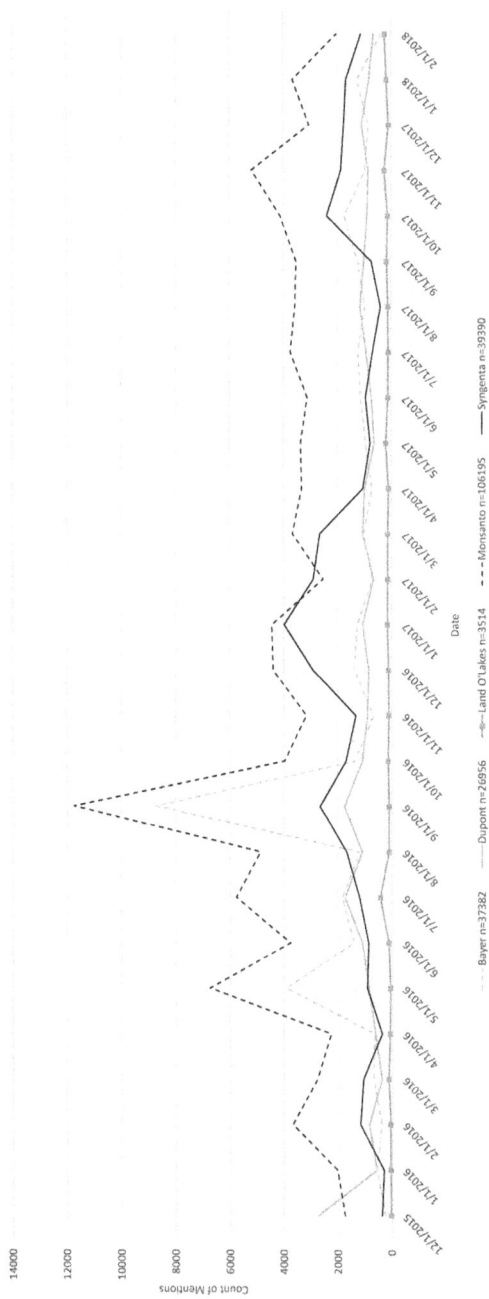

FIGURE 8.1. Monthly Mentions of Agribusiness Companies

Count of Mentions

14000

12000

10000

8000

6000

4000

2000

0

Date

12/1/2015, 1/1/2016, 2/1/2016, 3/1/2016, 4/1/2016, 5/1/2016, 6/1/2016, 7/1/2016, 8/1/2016, 9/1/2016, 10/1/2016, 11/1/2016, 12/1/2016, 1/1/2017, 2/1/2017, 3/1/2017, 4/1/2017, 5/1/2017, 6/1/2017, 7/1/2017, 8/1/2017, 9/1/2017, 10/1/2017, 11/1/2017, 1/1/2018, 3/1/2018

Bayer n=37382 — Dupont n=26956 — Land O'Lakes n=3514 — — Monsanto n=106195 — Syngenta n=39390

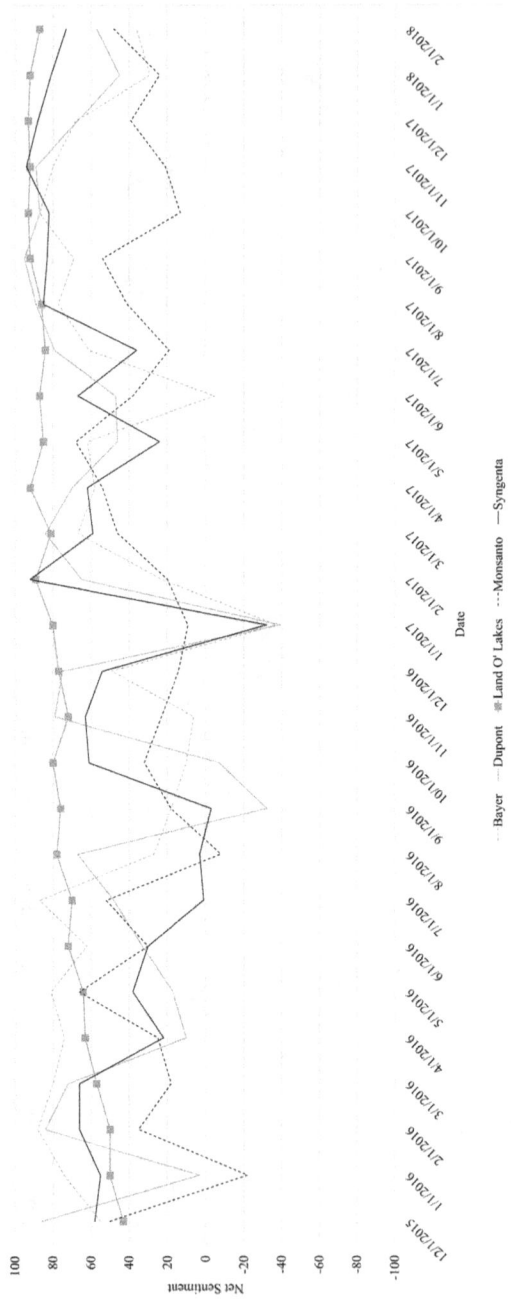

FIGURE 8.2. Net Sentiment of Online Mentions of Agribusiness Companies

As online and social media continue to evolve, so too do their impacts on agribusiness. Social media use overall has been increasing, yet penetration in agribusinesses has lagged behind other B2B industries. Nonetheless, there is a large volume of untapped data that could be analyzed to provide insights for agricultural firms. Particularly when a serious public relations issue happens, figuring out how fast and perhaps why something goes viral may provide brand management opportunities. Improved surveillance could help communicators in agricultural industries glean valuable insights about their public image and respond to concerns in a timely manner.

That said, the credibility of social media analytics depends on search term design, sentiment analysis accuracy, slang or vernacular interpretation, and data aggregation levels. For example, if positive sentiment is mostly driven by a company's own posts, it may conceal negative sentiment coming from outside the company. Monthly averaged sentiment may also be misguided if there is another incident happening in a certain week or a day of the month, considering the fast-changing nature of social media data.

Agricultural firms can draw broad but useful and timely inferences from aggregated sentiment data. Social listening complements traditional methods of measuring customer opinions, such as surveys and focus groups. As online media data becomes more common and multi-source datasets are amassed, analysis beyond the descriptive is possible. Additional data analysis that is more disaggregated on time, venue, and ownership will unlock more potential for social listening strategies and firm-level brand management.

WORKS CITED

Bunge, Jacob. 2014. "DuPont Sees $500 Million in Annual Revenue From Farm-Data Services." *wsj.com.* February 27. https://www.wsj.com/articles/dupont-sees-500-million-in-annual-revenue-from-farm-data-services-1393515676.

Campbell, Lisa, and Lisa R. Burchi. 2016. "Syngenta Settles with EPA on Alleged Label Violations." *lawbc.com.* September 19. https://www.lawbc.com/syngenta-settles-with-epa-on-alleged-label-violations/.

Cassidy, Emily. 2016. "Monsanto's New GMOs Spawn Illegal Use of Toxic Herbicides." *ewg.org.* August 3. https://www.ewg.org/news-insights/news/monsantos-new-gmos-spawn-illegal-use-toxic-herbicides.

Charles, Dan. 2016. "How Monsanto and Scofflaw Farmers Hurt Soybeans in Arkansas." *npr.com.* August 1. https://www.npr.org/sections/thesalt/2016/08/01/487809643/crime-in-the-fields-how-monsanto-and-scofflaw-farmers-hurt-soybeans-in-arkansas.

Davies, Steve. 2016. "Syngenta to Pay $1.2 M for Selling Misbranded Pesticides." *agri-pulse.com.* September 16. https://www.agri-pulse.com/articles/7487-syngenta-to-pay-1-2-m-for-selling-misbranded-pesticides.

Hakim, Danny. 2016. "Scientists Loved and Loathed by an Agrochemical Giant." *nytimes.com/2016.* December 31. https://www.nytimes.com/2016/12/31/business/scientists-loved-and-loathed-by-syngenta-an-agrochemical-giant.html.

Megaw, Nicholas. 2017. "Bayer Shares Drop After Profit Warning." *Financial Times.* July 27. https://www.ft.com/content/fac31c05-3d0d-380e-b7d0-db50bab80770.

Orpurt, Steven. 2016. "Monsanto's SEC Penalty for Improper Rebate Accounting." *businessjournalism.org.* March 28. https://businessjournalism.org/2016/03/monsanto/.

Philpott, Tom. 2016. "Monsanto Just Made a Massive Mistake." *motherjones.com/environment.* August 17. https://www.motherjones.com/environment/2016/08/monsanto-mistake-dicamba/.

Rehman, Shoaib Ur. 2017. "Bayer Stock Plunges on Profit Warning." *Business Recorder.* June 30. https://www.brecorder.com/news/356546/.

SEC. 2016. "Monsanto Paying $80 Million Penalty for Accounting Violations." *sec.gov.* https://www.sec.gov/newsroom/press-releases/2016-25.

Tullo, Alexander H. 2016. "DuPont Pension Changes Rattle Ex-Employees." *cen.acs.org/articles.* September 5. https://cen.acs.org/articles/94/i35/DuPont-pension-changes-rattle-ex.html.

Adapted from original posting as *ConsumerCorner.2021.Letter.6* (https://agribusiness.purdue.edu/consumer_corner/media-about-agribusiness-is-happening/)

9

#FOODSAFETY IN ONLINE MEDIA SPACE

BY JINHO JUNG, NICOLE J. OLYNK WIDMAR, AND COURTNEY BIR

H aving spent the past few chapters discussing the utility of engaging in online conversation (or at the very least, monitoring it), we now offer a series of case studies. Beyond private interest, social media can be seen as a catalyst for understanding public perceptions today because it has become the new "public square" of the modern, digital world.

As described in chapter 5, our ultimate interest in online media data lies in the realm of "public data for the public good," which led us to study foodborne illness outbreaks using online media data. Agricultural economists have long studied market and public reactions to food recall announcements, generally finding very small effects of recalls on consumer demand. We recently published an article in the *Journal of Food Protection* revealing that topical mentions in online and social media searches moved more closely in step with foodborne illness outbreak reports from the Centers for Disease Control (CDC) than with recall announcements by the US Food and Drug Administration (FDA) and the Food Safety Inspection Service (FSIS) (Jung et al. 2021) (see Figure 9.1).

When looking to see which group's recalls align more closely with online media mentions, we find a stronger correlation between CDC reports and online media data than between online media data and food recalls. We found that "this relative popularity reflects people more often

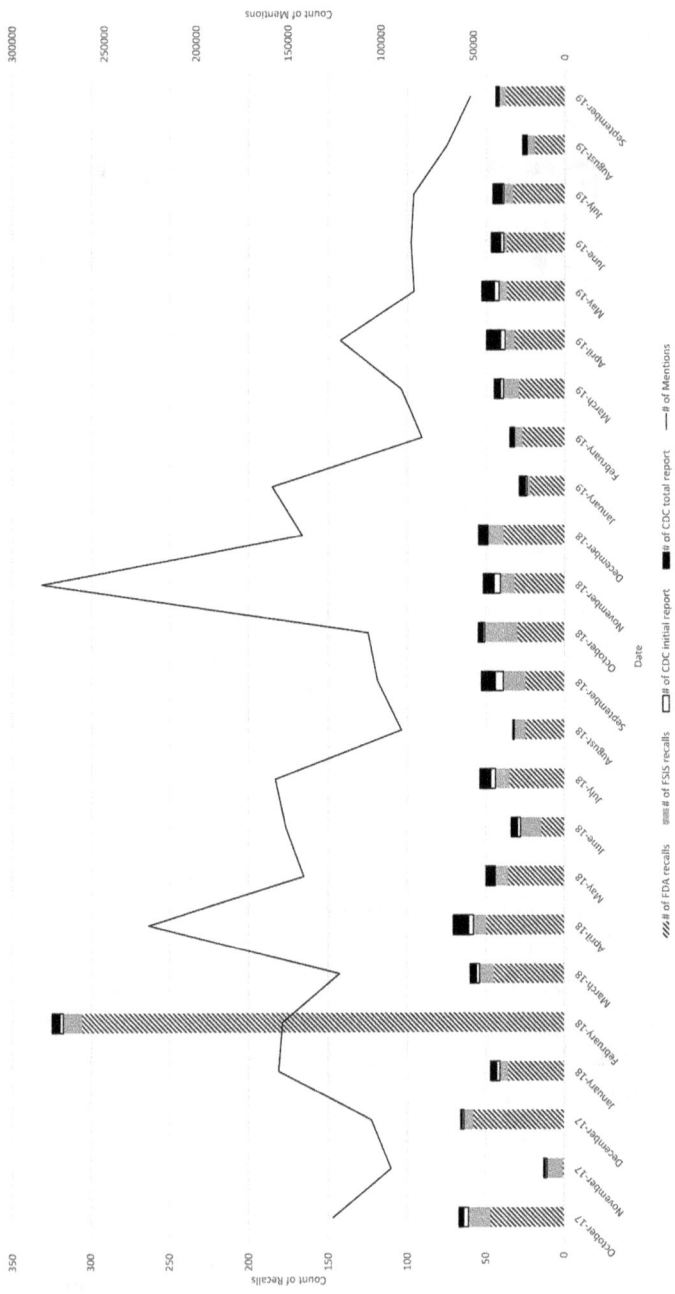

FIGURE 9.1. Online Media Mentions and Count of Recalls

sharing or posting about illness risk regardless of whether a recall occurs, suggesting that recall announcements by the FDA and FSIS may not induce changes in consumers' behavior, whereas initial illness reports by the CDC may" (Jung et al. 2021).

In addition, there is a lag in time between CDC illness reports and the eventual recall announcements by the FDA or FSIS, due to the several steps involved in foodborne outbreak investigation. Admittedly, CDC illness reports alert people of a "real and present threat" that warrants immediate attention, while the primary role of a recall is to remove potentially unsafe items from the store shelves after an investigation. Publicly available and publicly generated data, at least in the case of social media data, may offer policymakers insight into effective food risk communication in modern times, when much of our communication and information sharing is rapid and almost always online.

WORK CITED

Jung, Jinho, Courtney Bir, Nicole J. Olynk Widmar, and Peter Sayal. 2021. "Initial Reports of Foodborne Illness Drive More Public Attention Than Do Food Recall Announcements." *Journal of Food Protection* 1150–1159.

Adapted from original posting as *ConsumerCorner.2021.Letter.28* (https://www.agribusiness.purdue.edu/consumer_corner/food-safety-in -online-media-space/)

10

EVERYTHING IS ONLINE, EVEN YOUR GROCERIES

BY NICOLE J. OLYNK WIDMAR AND COURTNEY BIR

G rocery shopping has changed. Granted, there are new food products and flavors, varieties, and packages for seemingly every taste and preference on the shelves, but the groceries themselves are one thing. How you get them—from selecting items to paying for them to getting them into your cupboards at home has changed dramatically. Taking some liberty with an oversimplification here: We used to go to the store to get groceries. Now, we don't need to go to the store; we have options for using an app, a website, a third-party platform that facilitates shopping and delivery, Amazon, or a multitude of other online and/or brick-and-mortar-turned-online retailers. And that's just for selection.

When it comes to how food gets into your home, you have in-store pickup, curbside pickup, delivery by the retailer, delivery by a third party, or delivery via mail. This diversification in the final mile of food getting to households was underway long before 2020, but the COVID-19 pandemic fundamentally altered how we shop for and receive goods, including groceries, and accelerated these changes (Widmar et al. 2025). Even assessment of our food purchases has evolved with online procurement now facilitating reviews for grocery items that other shoppers can use to make decisions.

We asked 929 US residents about their online shopping habits and preferences in January 2021. We've quantified the online grocery shopping habits by type and frequency, finding use of different delivery methods varied in the time period studied—January 2020 through January 2021 (see Figure 10.1). Note that the (n) number provided in the figure reflects the number of respondents who reported participating in that type of grocery shopping activity out of our 929 total respondents.

Notably, the time period studied includes ten months of the COVID-19 pandemic, and respondents were surveyed immediately following the 2021 winter holiday season during which there were significant impacts on our behavior and well-being due to the pandemic (Widmar et al. 2025).

While we captured use of online grocery shopping at a particularly tumultuous point in time (January 2021), the real interest is in the changes in consumer behavior over time. Given the rapid changes seen in 2020, 2021, and continuing into 2022, the key question is about shopping intentions in the future. We found that 45 percent of our 929 respondents indicated they would be shopping for groceries online in the coming year.

BUT ARE YOU FOR OR AGAINST ONLINE GROCERY SHOPPING?

We've previously shared, in Book Three, some of our own pandemic practices that we kept postpandemic. Curbside pickup was a keeper for two of us, and another said they would continue shopping online but also visit stores for entertainment. Without a doubt, grocery shopping has changed, and consumer behaviors are sticky. The behaviors we've all adopted (even the weird canned goods and toilet paper hoarding ones) maybe stuck for some and even influenced how we behaved, just as significant and traumatic events did for others who came before us.

We recently tackled the proportion of US households shopping for groceries online and how they ultimately take ownership of those items, whether via delivery services, picking them up in-store, or through curbside service. In our January 2021 survey, we also explored why US households would and would not shop online moving forward. As noted earlier,

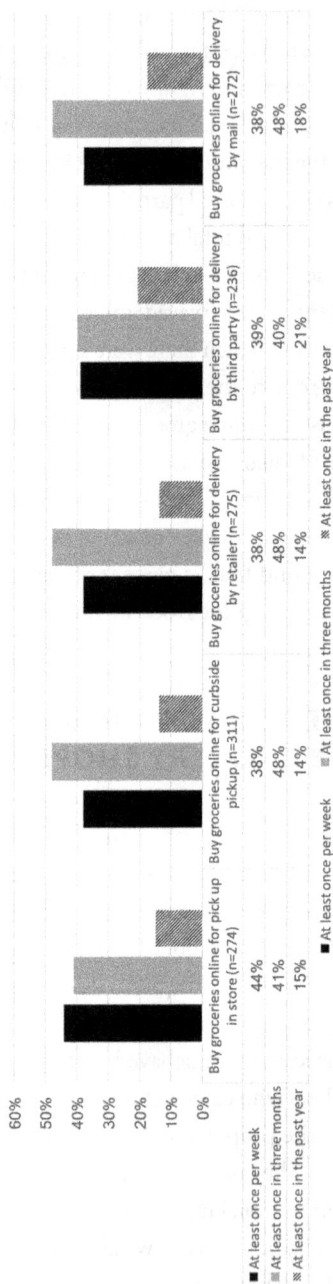

FIGURE 10.1. Online Grocery Shopping by Type and Frequency

	Buy groceries online for pick up in store (n=274)	Buy groceries online for curbside pickup (n=311)	Buy groceries online for delivery by retailer (n=275)	Buy groceries online for delivery by third party (n=236)	Buy groceries online for delivery by mail (n=272)
At least once per week	44%	38%	38%	39%	38%
At least once in three months	41%	48%	48%	40%	48%
At least once in the past year	15%	14%	14%	21%	18%

TABLE 10.1. *Why Respondents Would Shop Online for Groceries*

STATED PREFERENCE	% OF RESPONDENTS
Other reasons	8%
To lessen contact with other people due to COVID-19 or related health concerns	50%
To avoid impulse buying	22%
To save time	46%
Dislike of shopping in stores for groceries	10%
Due to physical constraints	10%
To access more stores and grocery items	17%
Because it is easier to shop for grocery items online	25%
To compare prices more easily	22%
To avoid lines	38%
Because I can easily choose delivery time	26%
Because I can order groceries anytime from anywhere	35%

Note: In the survey, 416 respondents were allowed to select more than one response.

and at the time of the survey, 45 percent of our 929 respondents said they would shop online in the coming year and 55 percent said they would not.

Top reasons for those who would shop online were to lessen contact with others due to COVID-19 concerns (50 percent); because it saves time (46 percent); and to avoid lines (38 percent). A close fourth was "I can order groceries anytime from anywhere"—which we highlight because it remains my (Nicole's) personal top reason still today. Early on, I was definitely avoiding unnecessary contact for safety (and I'm still more cautious than the average person), but the fact that I can add two or three items to my grocery list while I'm cooking, sitting in a waiting room, or simply remember something I need has fundamentally changed how I procure household items and food items. I don't know if I could go back to my "old way." If I had to, it would now be quite an adjustment.

Now switching gears to the majority of respondents: The top reasons cited by the 55 percent who said they *would not* shop online in the post-pandemic year were liking to see and choose products in person before buying (65 percent); enjoying shopping in-store (52 percent); and not

TABLE 10.2. *Reasons Respondents Would Not Shop Online for Groceries*

STATED PREFERENCE (RESPONDENTS MAY CHOOSE MORE THAN ONE)	% OF RESPONDENTS
Other reasons	4%
I do not trust online grocery retailers	18%
I have limited internet access	1%
Previous bad experience with online grocery shopping	5%
I find picking up orders at the store inconvenient	7%
Online grocery shopping is not available from any retailer in my area	2%
My favorite/preferred grocery retailer does not offer this service in my area	3%
I find it inconvenient waiting for delivery	15%
I do not like to plan my grocery shopping in advance	9%
I do not like paying for delivery/curbside	31%
I enjoy shopping for groceries in-store	52%
I like to see and choose the products in person before choosing them	65%

Note: In the survey, 513 respondents were allowed to select more than one response.

wanting to pay charges for delivery or curbside (31 percent). There are certain items like meat and produce I would have previously felt uncomfortable ordering online. This is one case in which COVID-19 forced me to stretch outside my comfort zone and try it. Now, I cannot imagine going back. Some of us are still enjoying free curbside service, whereas many are not or are paying the delivery charges.

Taken together, there are interesting changes in consumer behavior surrounding online grocery shopping. In fact, the reasons with the lowest percentages may be more revealing than those with the highest (or most popular). For example, only 9 percent of respondents said they don't shop online because they don't like to plan their shopping in advance. And only 5 percent indicated they had a previous bad experience. Meanwhile, 18 percent percent don't trust online grocery retailers, which may be an interesting point for further research: What do people consider an "online retailer" versus their trusted neighborhood store that also happens to offer online service? Without a doubt, we raise more questions than answers about how food and grocery items get into US households, but it seems the fundamental drivers of more online grocery shopping are there, and many of the reasons not to shop online may be surmountable with enough time, trust, and effort by retailers.

WORK CITED

Widmar, Nicole J. Olynk, Michael L. Smith, and Erin Robinson. 2025. *Consumer Corner: Consumer Lessons from a Pandemic.* Purdue University Press.

Adapted from original posting as *ConsumerCorner.2022.Letter.10* and *ConsumerCorner.2022.Letter.11* (https://agribusiness.purdue.edu/consumer_corner/everything-is-online -even-your-groceries/ and https://agribusiness.purdue.edu/consumer _corner/are-you-for-or-against-online-grocery-shopping/)

11

DID YOU KNOW THAT FLOUR IS RAW?

BY JINHO JUNG

I
n chapter 9 we discussed online and social media analytics surrounding food safety by relating food recall announcements to their effect on consumer demand. Now we turn to a more specific case. While chapter 9 considered foodborne illness outbreaks generally, our study, "Online Media Attention Devoted to Flour and Flour-Related Food Safety in 2017–2020," focuses on a specific product—flour—and its related food safety issues in the online and social media space (Jung et al. 2022). Even though flour can harbor disease-causing bacteria such as Shiga toxin–producing *Escherichia coli* (STEC) and salmonella, it is rarely perceived to be as risky as other raw commodities such as meat, eggs, and leafy vegetables (FDA 2024). In reality, between 2017 and 2019, two foodborne illness outbreaks in the United States were linked to the consumption of flour products: one involved 21 cases of STEC and the other 7 cases of Salmonella (Harris and Yada 2022).

Using online and social media analytics, we monitored the online media space and quantified both the share of media mentions and the net sentiment regarding flour and flour-related food safety risks from 2017 to 2020. We found 22 million timeline mentions for general flour searches, compared to 90,000 mentions related to flour-related illness. Notably, general flour searches fluctuated seasonally, often increasing ahead of the holiday season (November–December) (Figure 11.1). A prominent, rapid,

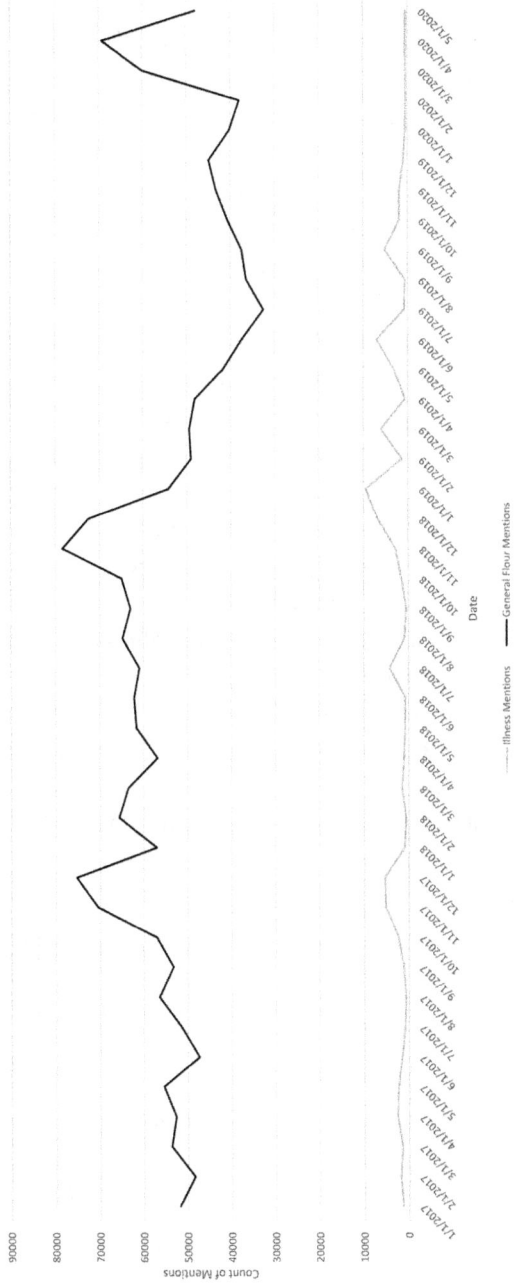

FIGURE 11.1. Monthly Mentions in the General Flour and the Flour-Related Illness Searches

and unusual increase in the volume of mentions happened in March 2020 (Figure 11.1). Considering that top-searched words during the month were "home baking" and "cooking" within posts also mentioning "quarantine," the rise in volume may be related to the COVID-19 pandemic and stay-at-home orders.

Although the dataset for flour-related illness (90,000 mentions) is smaller than the general flour (22 million mentions) dataset, accounting for less than 1 percent, search results collected accurately reflected initial CDC reports and all the FDA's flour recalls in real time (Figure 11.2 and Table 11.1).

Monthly net sentiment also changed over time (Figure 11.3). The changes were more significant for flour-related illness searches—which were mostly negative—while they were positive for the general flour searches (Figure 11.3). Given that flour-related illnesses cause acute symptoms and discomfort, these negative net sentiment results were expected.

The top five attributes that drive positive and negative sentiments are also presented for both the general flour search and flour-related illness searches (Table 11.2 and Table 11.3). Flour-related illness net sentiment was mostly driven by terms like "kill bacterium" (positive) and "recall" (negative). On the other hand, net sentiment from the general flour search results varied and mostly related to activities with flour such as baking.

The *Consumer Corner* letter from which we share this information is based on the publication "Online Media Attention Devoted to Flour and Flour-Related Food Safety in 2017 to 2020," by Jinho Jung, Nicole J. Olynk Widmar, Sangavi Subramani, and Yaohua Feng. The paper was published (January 2022) in the *Journal of Food Protection* and is available at https:// doi.org/10.4315/JFP-21-085.

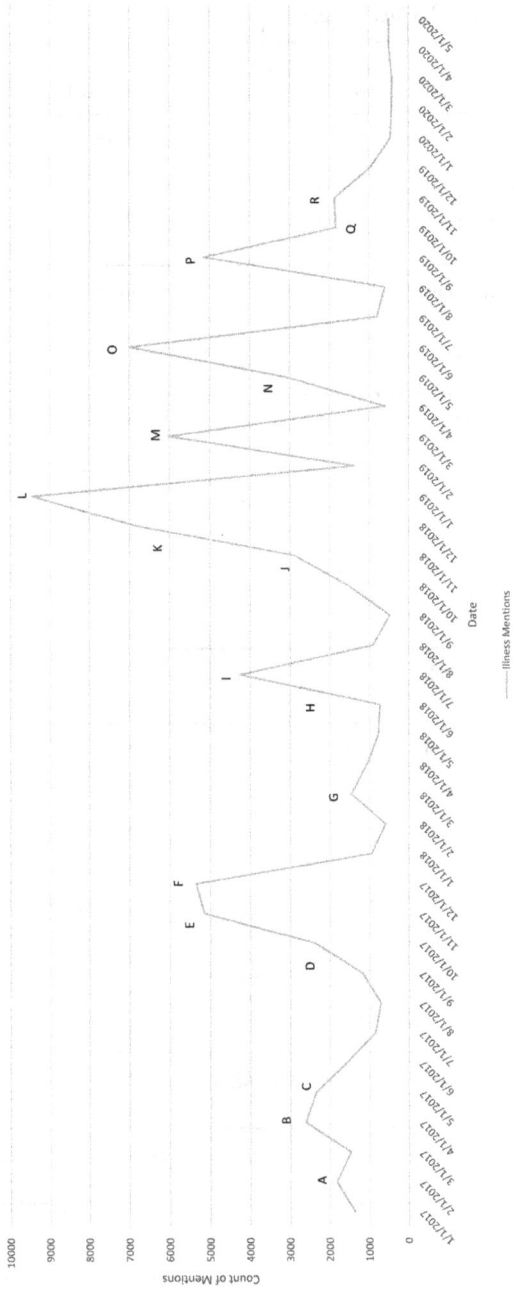

FIGURE 11.2. Monthly Mentions for Flour-Related Illness Searches Labeled with FDA Flour Product Recalls, 2018–2020

TABLE 11.1. *List of FDA Flour Product Recalls, 2018–2020*

PRODUCT	PATHOGEN	DATE OF PUBLIC ANNOUNCEMENT	FDA'S NOTIFICATION	RECALLED?	SOURCE, FDA
King Arthur organic coconut flour	Salmonella	03/23/2018 - G	4/7/2018	Yes	2018
Bob's Red Mill Organic Amaranth flour	Salmonella	04/06/2018 - G	4/7/2018	Yes	2018
Duncan Hines Classic Cake: White, Yellow, Butter Golden, Signature Confetti (cake mixes)	Salmonella	11/05/2018 - J	#######	No	2018
Gold Medal unbleached all-purpose flour	Salmonella	01/23/2019 - L	2/1/2019	Yes	2019
Pillsbury Best unbleached all-purpose flour	Salmonella	03/13/2019 - M	#######	Yes	2019
Baker's Corner all-purpose flour	E. coli	05/23/2019 - N	#######	Yes	2019
King Arthur unbleached all-purpose flour	E. coli	06/13/2019 - O	#######	Yes	2019
Pillsbury Best bread flour	E. coli	06/14/2019 - O	#######	Yes	2019
Brand Castle, Sisters Gourmet, In the Mix cookie and brownie mixes	E. coli	06/21/2019 - O	#######	Yes	2019
Gold Medal unbleached all-purpose flour	E. coli O26	09/16/2019 - P	#######	Yes	2019
King Arthur unbleached all-purpose flour	E. coli O26	10/03/2019 - Q	#######	Yes	2019
Robin Hood all-purpose flour	E. coli	10/04/2019 - Q	#######	Yes	2019
Wild Harvest organic all-purpose flour	E. coli	11/27/2019 - R	#######	Yes	2019
Hodgson Mill unbleached flour	E. coli	11/27/2019 - R	#######	Yes	2019

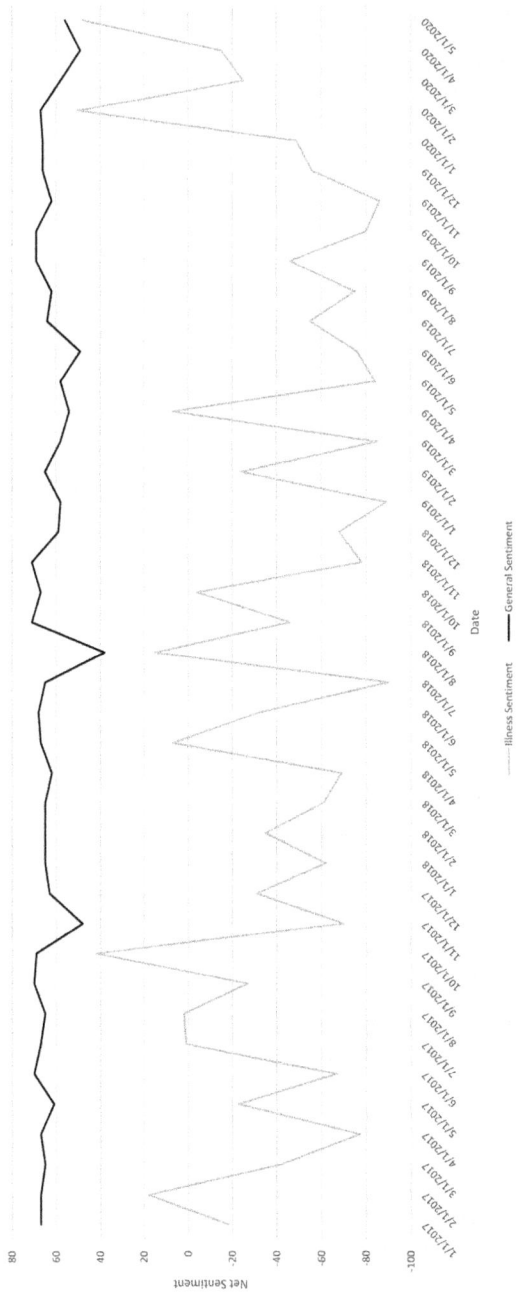

FIGURE 11.3. Monthly Net Sentiment in the General Flour and Flour-Related Illness Searches

TABLE 11.2. *Sentiment Drivers for the General Flour Search*

TERM	SENTIMENT SCORE	TERM	SENTIMENT SCORE
Expensive	−4%	Awesome baking	5%
Not work	−4%	Great British Baking Show	6%
Recall	−10%	Easy	7%
Too thick	−18%	Fresh	12%
Too runny	−18%	Great British Baking Show	24%

TABLE 11.3. *Sentiment Drivers for the Flour-Related Illness Search*

TERM	SENTIMENT SCORE	TERM	SENTIMENT SCORE
contaminate with *E. coli*	−4%	treated flour	4%
bacterium	−7%	Pillsbury Best Bread Flour	4%
contaminate with bacterium	−7%	safe to eat	5%
afraid of salmonella	−14%	worth risk	8%
recall	−38%	kill bacterium	43%

WORKS CITED

FDA. 2024. "Handling Flour Safely: What You Need to Know." *fda.gov/food.* March 5. Accessed 2025. https://www.fda.gov/food/buy-store-serve-safe-food /handling-flour-safely-what-you-need-know.

Harris, L. J., and Yada, S. 2022. "Flour and Cereal Grain Products: Foodborne Illness Outbreaks and Product Recalls [Tables and References]." *Flour & Cereal Grains—Outbreaks and Recalls.*

Jung, Jinho, Nicole J. Olynk Widmar, Sangavi Subramani, and Yaohua Feng. 2022. "Online Media Attention Devoted to Flour and Flour-Related Food Safety in 2017 to 2020." *Journal of Food Protection* 73–84.

Adapted from original posting as *ConsumerCorner.2022.Letter.13* (https://agribusiness.purdue.edu/consumer_corner/did-you-know-that -flour-is-raw/)

12

WHAT WAS ON THE CHOPPING BLOCK FOR EASTER 2022?

B ack in 2014, I first studied and reported on holiday meal meat choices, focusing on the Thanksgiving turkey. Since then, we've kept talking, revisiting our turkey preferences during the pandemic (remember the smaller turkeys for smaller gatherings?) and discussing supply issues in 2021. In January 2021, we reflected on the 2020 holiday season from a meat proteins standpoint. That season was shaped by COVID-era supply chain disruptions that impacted some cuts of meats more than others.

But then we accepted that the 2019 version of "normal" is never coming back. We've moved past the idea of "returning to normal" and shifted toward living today—and planning for the future. By the spring of 2022, some supply chain problems were still lingering, while others seemed to be easing, setting the stage for a less strained path ahead.

In a completely nonscientific, not at all representative, and entirely "just for fun" Twitter poll conducted right before Easter, I asked what protein was being served. With an admittedly very small sample size, pork or Easter ham was the clear winner. We know turkey is the star of the

TABLE 12.1. *Which Protein Is at the Center of Your Table This Easter Weekend?*

RESPONSE	% OF RESPONDENTS
Beef	9.1%
Pork or Ham	72.7%
Poultry	4.5%
Nonmeat proteins	13.6%

Total out of 22 votes in a poll conducted via Twitter online.

TABLE 12.2. *How Does This Year's Easter Main Course Compare to Previous Years?*

RESPONSE	% OF RESPONDENTS
Unchanged; same as always	85.7%
Unchanged because of prices	0%
Changed because of availability	7.1%
Changed for other reasons	7.1%

Total out of 14 votes in a poll conducted via Twitter online.

table at Thanksgiving, and at least in my certainly biased and admittedly too-tiny Twitter following, the Easter ham still reigns supreme for this particular holiday.

Perhaps even more interesting (in terms of overall consumer behavior) was how few people said they were changing their Easter meal plans due to price, availability, or other concerns. Again, this was just a small, casual poll—but 85 percent reported sticking to their usual menu.

We've talked a lot about changing meat prices in recent years. From rising beef costs to the inconvenient reality that you can't get more chicken wings without producing more chickens, the meat case has been anything but boring. Pandemic-related ripple effects—like restaurant closures, increased at-home cooking, retail food demand, and school closures—all put pressure on meat protein supply chains. Back in Book Three, we had some stern words about consumers under duress during COVID and then argued that our learned behaviors during the pandemic were likely to be stickier than we might want to admit.

In total, *Consumer Corner* debuted over 20 pieces about consumer behaviors during COVID-19, all compiled in Book Three. Although I'm certainly not drawing any grand conclusions from a handful of Twitter polls, it does make me wonder: Which behaviors are truly sticky (like stockpiling toilet paper)? And which ones are more resistant to change—especially when they're tightly held to long-standing traditions, like holiday meals?

It seems like the how, when, and who of our tightly held holiday rituals are among the most resilient of our consumer behaviors. Even though we adapted our celebrations in 2020, maybe those holidays proved more durable than many of us expected. Time will tell.

———————

Adapted from original posting as *ConsumerCorner.2022.Letter.14* (https://agribusiness.purdue.edu/consumer_corner/what-was-on-the -chopping-block-for-easter-2022/)

13

#HALLOWEEN THROUGH THE YEARS

BY NICOLE J. OLYNK WIDMAR AND COURTNEY BIR

H alloween, born of All Hallow's Eve, is an annual ritual in the United States that brings communities together. *Consumer Corner* has made a (nearly) annual tradition of examining public opinions on Halloween. Recall Halloween in 2021—by then, we were tired of comparing ourselves to pre-pandemic normalcy, but we were ready to chart our path forward into the next frontier . . . we think. Negative comments in 2020 were obviously pandemic-related, with the top two negatives from nearly five million mentions in October 2020 being "not worth getting sick" and "COVID." Yet, net sentiment went from 78 percent in October 2019 to 81 percent in 2020. While we were collectively concerned, we were also (apparently) motivated to adapt and generally expressed more positive online media sentiment surrounding Halloween 2020 relative to 2019.

On October 25, 2021, we opened our polling question and asked readers to weigh in on whether national online and social media sentiment toward Halloween 2021 was going to be better or worse than in 2020. The ($n = 22$) responses have been tallied. As it turns out, *Consumer Corner* enthusiasts are an optimistic bunch: 45 percent thought Halloween 2021 would have a much better sentiment surrounding it than Halloween 2020; 25 percent expected Halloween 2021 to be a little better; 16 percent expected the same;

and 20 percent expected a little worse. A whopping 0 percent of respondents expected a "much worse" experience in 2021 compared to 2020. Now, admittedly, it was a loaded question. After all, we asked people to compare 2021 to the year in which the most positive emblem remains toilet paper.

Overall, *Consumer Corner* readers were optimistic about 2021. Net sentiment for October 2021 came in at 81 percent, which is identical to what was posted for October 2020 (remember, net sentiment is on a scale of -100 percent to +100 percent, so 81 percent is quite high).

Looking at 2021 data, which again employed the same straightforward and intentionally constrained set of keywords (Halloween, #Halloween, Trick-or-Treat, #TrickorTreat, Trunk-or-Treat, #TrunkorTreat, and #Halloween2021), the overall mentions (or volume of data) were down only slightly—October 2021 came within 5,000 mentions of the prior year.

The volume of media really didn't change from 2020—and, surprisingly, neither did net sentiment. What did change were the topics of conversation and the top words driving that sentiment. Top terms in 2020 were almost all COVID-19 related: "not worth getting sick," "COVID," and lots (and lots!) of positivity around making Halloween safe or safer. In contrast, 2021's top terms were less pandemic-focused and more Halloween-centered. "Happy Halloween" and the pumpkin emoji were the top positive drivers, while the negative drivers included "scary" and references of scary or difficult "costumes."

Perhaps surprisingly, two of the top three positive drivers were emojis: the pumpkin (🎃) being second and the cute, friendly ghost (👻) being third.

Halloween 2022: With the *Wall Street Journal* headlines like "Soaring Inflation Pushes Halloween Candy Prices Scary High" leading the week ahead of Halloween 2022, there was concern about whether rising prices would put a damper on the festivities (Lukpat 2022). Given

TABLE 13.1. *Volume of October Mentions by Year*

	OCTOBER 2019	OCTOBER 2020	OCTOBER 2021
Volume of Mentions	6,701,716	4,889,455	4,884,434
Net Sentiment	+78	+81	+81

the pre-holiday jitters in 2022, we wondered what that year's sentiment would be surrounding Halloween. For 2022, it was a "Happy Halloween" after all. Net sentiment was high at 80 percent, and the top conversations were focused on Halloween fun, with little widespread chatter about the associated costs.

Halloween 2023: Halloween in 2023 really *was* happy. "Happy Halloween" was the top term used overall on social media. With Halloween 2023 reaching an 85 percent sentiment overall, it was the highest we had seen in years. The previous year it was only a Happy Halloween "after all." Despite fears of expensive (thanks, inflation!) candy dampening the fun, the overall sentiment was high at 80 percent in 2022 (Ellison 2022). Fast forward to 2023 and gone were the lingering mentions of pandemic-era caution. Instead, Halloween was back—fun, festive, and full of emojis.

Much like Friendsgiving has expanded Thanksgiving into a month-long celebration, is the car trunk our new excuse for weeks-long sugary extravaganzas? Mentions of "trunk-or-treat" suggest that might be the case. For example, our family trunk-or-treated with glee as early as October 14 . . . then faced a snowstorm on October 31 and reminded the children, "We *already* went trick-or-treating, remember?!" #Genius?

Looking at total media volume surrounding Halloween, a distinct pattern emerges, peaking precisely on October 31. Yet, the mid-month "trunk" spike raised a question: Is Halloween creeping in earlier? Holiday creep for the creepiest holiday?

Holiday creep is nothing new, really. Home Depot had trees and elves out on display in late October, wreaking havoc for anyone trying to navigate the store with children and without Santa's presence sixty days ahead of time (ask me how I know). Maybe more time to celebrate is a good thing? Maybe it matters which holiday we're talking about?

"Where do you think you're going? Nobody's leaving. Nobody's walking out on this fun, old-fashioned family Christmas. No, no. We're all in this together. This is a full-blown, four-alarm holiday emergency here. We're gonna press on, and we're gonna have the hap, hap, happiest Christmas."

You should be able to name that movie quote. If not, you have some serious work to do.

Answer: Clark Griswold in *Christmas Vacation*.

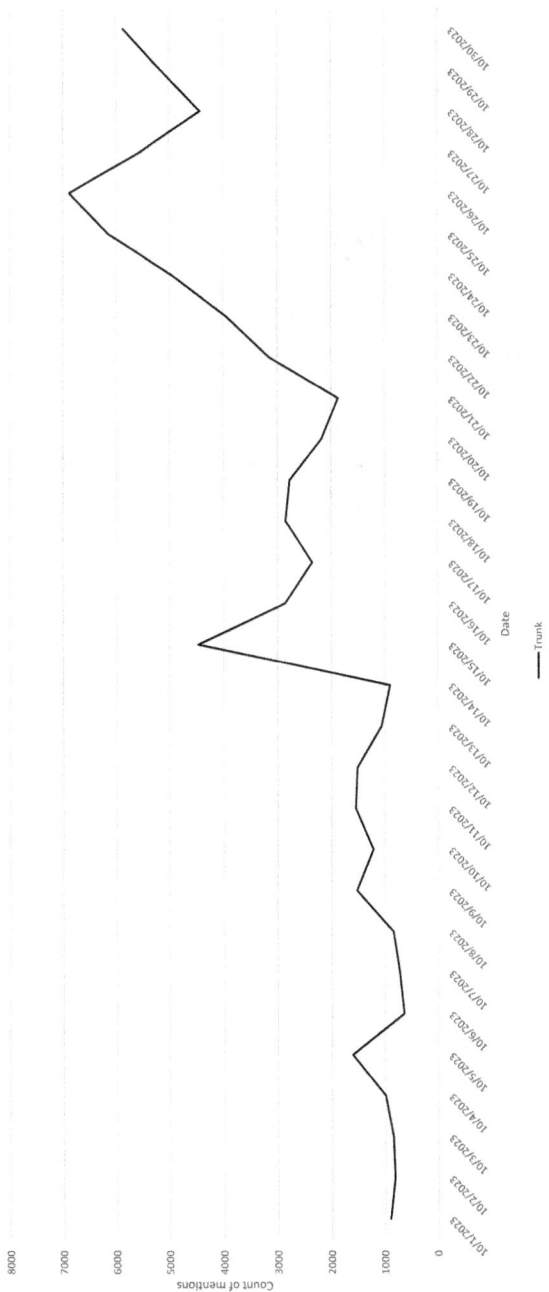

FIGURE 13.1. Mentions of "Trunk or Treat" in October 2023

TABLE 13.2. *Online Media Net Sentiments on Halloween*

	2019	2020	2021	2022	2023
Net Sentiment	78	81	81	80	85

WORKS CITED

Ellison, Jillian. 2022. "It Was a 'Happy Halloween' After All, Purdue Professor Explains." *purdue.edu/news*. November 1. https://ag.purdue.edu/news/2022/11/it-was-a-happy-halloween-after-all-purdue-professor-explains.html.

Lukpat, Alyssa. 2022. "Soaring Inflation Pushes Halloween Candy Prices Scary High." *wsj.com/articles*. October 25. https://www.wsj.com/articles/soaring-inflation-pushes-halloween-candy-prices-scary-high-11666643954.

Adapted from original postings as *Consumer.Corner.2021.Article.10*, *ConsumerCorner.2022.Letter.41*, and *ConsumerCorner.2023.Letter.27* (https://agribusiness.purdue.edu/consumer_corner/halloween2021/, https://agribusiness.purdue.edu/consumer_corner/halloween2022/, https://agribusiness.purdue.edu/consumer_corner/happyhalloween2023-thats-a-wrap/)

14

WE ARE ALL
A BUNCH OF LIARS

I n Book One of this series, we talked about how you were a hypo-
crite (Book One, chapter 3). And you still are (sorry to be the one to
tell you). Later in that same book (chapter 10), we talked about your
YouTube-worthy temper tantrums and why they need to stop. In *Consumer
Corner's* online format, we welcomed 2022 by calling you a liar (Widmar
and Bir 2022a). In fairness, the title was *Well, You're Also a Liar*, implying
that it isn't just you, it's us too.

We know that most of us keep everything on the internet. We live on
the internet and probably have an Apple Watch strapped to our wrists to
complement the functionality of the iPhone clutched in our hands. I mean,
Have You Hugged Your iPhone Today was one of our favorite *Consumer Corner* posts from 2021 (Widmar 2021a).

Trying to understand human behavior, how people make decisions and
why, is what we do on *Consumer Corner*, using a variety of data sources.
Surveys are valuable in designing questions about specific topics, such as
when we looked into preferences for public versus private control of things
like military services and education (Young 2022). But surveys do have a
variety of challenges, from ensuring adequate sample size to conduct the
analyses desired, to worrying about response bias, enumerator bias, and a

whole slew of other biases when asking questions that people know are being analyzed by other people (even if anonymously) (Widmar 2022a).

Online and social media data is (at least in my opinion) the new frontier. It exists in a variety of forms—from tweets about holiday plans to smart devices in your home. Social media data has been analyzed to explore public understanding of public health crises like the Zika virus and to question whether natural disasters with more social media coverage receive more aid or funding (answer is: they do not) (Widmar and Bir 2022b). But social media has its challenges too. You post your best life on Twitter, you might say things that do not accurately reflect how you *really* feel, and not everyone is represented. In short, all datasets have challenges, and social media is no exception.

There is an online data set that knows more about us than social media ever could. It's that little bar at the top of your screen—the one that that knows our deepest secrets, even the really unflattering stuff. The stuff that would (and probably *should*) make other people recoil if they saw it. That little bar? It's the Google search bar. And the resulting Google search data.

Seth Stephens-Davidowitz's book *Everybody Lies: Big Data, New Data, and What the Internet Can Tell Us About Who We Really Are* delves into a variety of topics using Google search data (Stephens-Davidowitz 2017). He used Google Trends for much of his work, augmenting it with Google AdWords data and his own algorithm (described in detail in his dissertation and journal article "The Cost of Racial Animus on a Black Presidential Candidate: Using Google Search Data to Find What Surveys Miss"; Stephens-Davidowitz 2013). The bottom line is that people tell Google things they might not tell anyone else; not their friends, their spouse, or their doctor.

Seth also posits (and we tend to agree with him) that search data may reveal lies we even tell ourselves. So it's not that we lie to others—we lie to ourselves, too. Given how well Google search data seems to reflect reality (often more accurately than surveys), it's safe to say that we do not lie to Google (or at least not nearly as much). Seth Stephens-Davidowitz worked at Google as a data scientist after they became aware of his research on racism using Google search data. His features in the *New York*

Times included pieces such as "How Racist Are We? Ask Google," "The Data of Hate," and "Searching for Sex" (Stephens-Davidowitz 2012, 2014, 2015). His book explores topics from mental illness to sexuality, child abuse to religion. Not surprisingly, these highly sensitive and emotional topics are notoriously difficult to study using survey data. Also not surprisingly, these topics receive a lot of attention in Google searches. On page 14, he writes, "I am now convinced that Google searches are the most important dataset ever collected on the human psyche" (Stephens-Davidowitz 2017).

The book is presented in three parts:

- Part I: "Data, Big and Small"
- Part II: "The Powers of Big Data"
- Part III: "Big Data: Handle with Care"

The conclusion is aptly titled "How Many People Finish Books" and suggests the answer is not very many. But it's a strong conclusion and worth the read.

Chapter 8, titled "Mo Data, Mo Problems? What We Shouldn't Do," opens with: "Sometimes, the power of Big Data is so impressive it's scary. It raises ethical questions." He argues there is danger in data-empowered corporations learning what customers can or will pay—or how to exploit them. Gambling is highlighted as a particularly risky space, as firms seek to maximize profit off very personal behavior insights. Gambling is, after all, a treasure trove for studying human behavior, which we've also examined in the context of data-driven decision (or lack thereof) (Widmar 2022b).

Seth says on page 265: "Data on the internet, in other words, can tell businesses which customers to avoid and which they can exploit. It can also tell customers the businesses they should avoid and who is trying to exploit them. Big Data to date has helped both sides in the struggle between consumers and corporations. We have to make sure it remains a fair fight."

There is a lot to gain from understanding ourselves and our societies through new data sources. Data use remains a question nearly every industry is grappling with. We've argued before that big data itself is a challenge, but its use is a wicked problem (Widmar 2021b).

On page 270, Stephens-Davidowitz cautions: "So we have to be really cautious about allowing the government to intervene at the individual level based on search data. This is not just for ethical or legal reasons. It's also, at least for now, for data science reasons."

Really, it's not just the government. Any entity faces ethical, legal, and technical reasons to question data use, especially at the individual level. Given the power in online data, and especially search data, I suspect that the question of use will only grow more complicated as the possibilities continue to expand for what's possible within these datasets.

WORKS CITED

Stephens-Davidowitz, Seth. 2012. "How Racist Are We? Ask Google." *nytimes .com.* June 9. https://archive.nytimes.com/campaignstops.blogs.nytimes.com /2012/06/09/how-racist-are-we-ask-google/.

Stephens-Davidowitz, Seth. 2013. *The Cost of Racial Animus on a Black Presidential Candidate: Using Google Search Data to Find What Surveys Miss.* SSRN.

Stephens-Davidowitz, Seth. 2014. "The Data of Hate." *nytimes.com.* July 12. https:// www.nytimes.com/2014/07/13/opinion/sunday/seth-stephens-davidowitz -the-data-of-hate.html.

Stephens-Davidowitz, Seth. 2015. "Searching for Sex." *nytimes.com.* January 24. https://www.nytimes.com/2015/01/25/opinion/sunday/seth-stephens -davidowitz-searching-for-sex.html?ref=opinion.

Stephens-Davidowitz, Seth. 2017. *Everybody Lies: Big Data, New Data, and What the Internet Can Tell Us About Who We Really Are.* Dey Street Books.

Widmar, Nicole Olynk. 2021a. "Have You Hugged Your iPhone Today?." *Consumer Corner.* May 24. https://agribusiness.purdue.edu/consumer_corner/have-you -hugged-your-iphone-today/.

Widmar, Nicole Olynk. 2021b. "'Big Data' in Animal Industries: Scale Is Chal- lenging, But Use Is Wicked." *Consumer Corner.* September 20. https:// agribusiness.purdue.edu/consumer_corner/big-data-in-animal-industries -scale-is-challenging/.

Widmar, Nicole Olynk. 2022a. "It's Worth Repeating, Sample Size Matters." *Con- sumer Corner.* August 15. https://agribusiness.purdue.edu/consumer_corner/its -worth-repeating-sample-size-matters/.

Widmar, Nicole Olynk. 2022b. "Everything Is Just Math." *Consumer Corner.* July 11. https://agribusiness.purdue.edu/consumer_corner/everything-is-just-math/.

Widmar, Nicole Olynk, and Courtney Bir. 2022a. "Well, You're Also a Liar." *Consumer Corner.* https://agribusiness.purdue.edu/consumer_corner/well-youre -also-a-liar/.

Widmar, Nicole Olynk, and Courtney Bir. 2022b. "Questioning the Value of 'Thoughts and Prayers' for Natural Disaster Victims." *Consumer Corner.* April 4. https://agribusiness.purdue.edu/consumer_corner/questioning-the-value-of -thoughts-and-prayers-for-natural-disaster-victims/.

Young, Jeffrey S. 2022. "Who's in Charge Here, Anyway?." *Consumer Corner.* February 22. https://agribusiness.purdue.edu/consumer_corner/whos-in-charge -here-anyway/.

Adapted from original posting as *ConsumerCorner.2022.Letter.37*
https://agribusiness.purdue.edu/2022/11/08/everybody-lies-big-data-new -data-and-what-the-internet-can-tell-us-about-who-we-really-are/

15

#BABYFORMULA

Based on Jung et al. (2022)

Y ou undoubtedly heard about, experienced, witnessed, or participated in the uncertainty, and ultimately panic, of the recent 2022 US
baby formula shortage. While you may have spent your 2022 sum-
mer road trip scouring out-of-town shelves for friends' formula needs (or
attempted to meet your own baby's formula needs), what you might not
have realized was that months before the May and June 2022 panic, there
were warnings (alarm bells, one might say) that went unheeded.

In February 2022, a voluntary recall was issued. The FDA announced
the recall and released information to consumers about how to identify re-
called products (FDA 2022). However, there was not a significant uptick in
online media about infant formula until May 2022, and, even then, the sud-
den attention on baby formula dissipated within three weeks, despite a con-
tinuous rise on out-of-stock rates in late May through mid-June. Formula
shortages continued into the fall of 2022, although media attention continued to lessen over time. This rapid fall in public interest—even while threats
persist (or increase)—has been documented before, including in coverage
of #Mosquitoes (see chapter 5) and #NaturalDisasters (Widmar and Bir
2022). The deterioration of online media attention while threats persist is a
known phenomenon. Yet, in this case, you may be surprised to learn that the
first public recognition of the threat was woefully late, and public attention
fell rapidly even as physical product shortages were still being widely faced.

As stated in the original article: "The infant formula situation could
have been somewhat mitigated if the supply chain warning in the FDA's

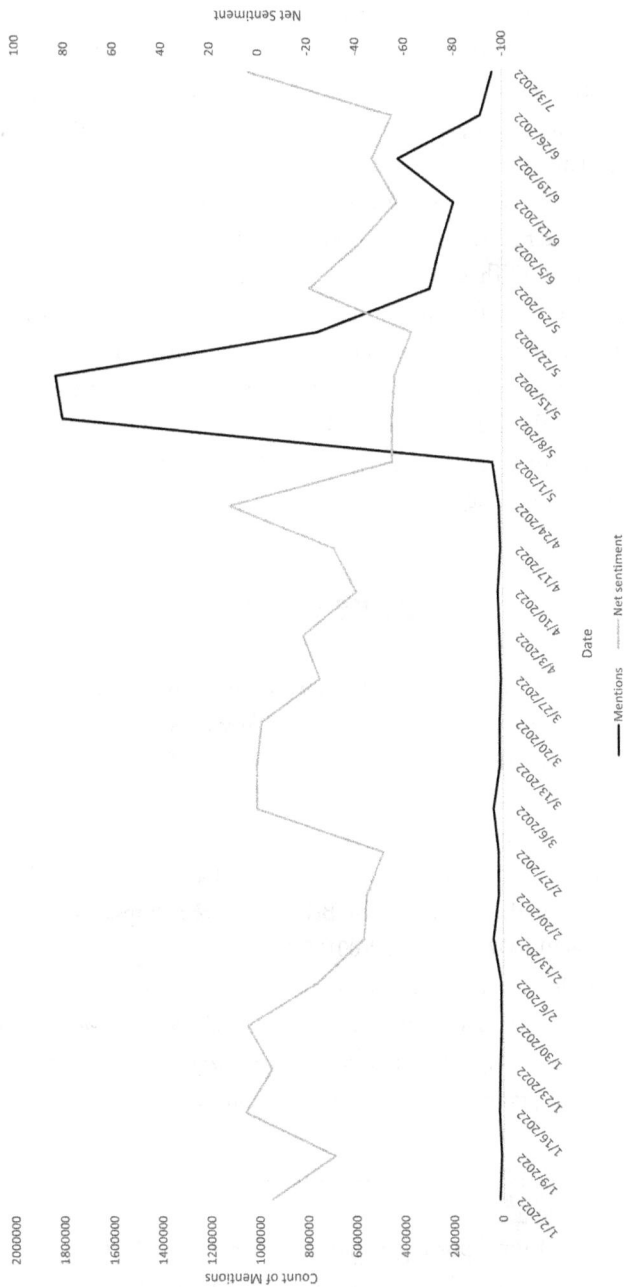

FIGURE 15.1. Mentions and Net Sentiment of Baby Formula. Adapted from Fig. 1 from Jung et al. 2022.

recall announcement would have been heeded by the public, related industries, and the government when the recall was first issued." And: "The lack of timely response, or even timely coverage and educational campaigns to help parents prepare, arguably worsened the panic when physical shortages occurred, seemingly without warning for many people" (Jung et al. 2022).

Given today's rapid dissemination of information and rampant (over) sharing on social media platforms, how was such an impactful recall largely missed for months? These were valuable months that could have been used to be sure of supplies (where possible), or at the very least, to inform and educate parents ahead of experiencing physical product shortages. From a public policy and communication standpoint, there are lessons to be learned from "The Curious Case of Baby Formula in the United States in 2022: Cries for Urgent Action Months After Silence in the Midst of Alarm Bells" (Jung et al. 2022).

WORKS CITED

FDA. 2022. "FDA Investigation of Cronobacter Infections: Powdered Infant Formula (February 2022)." August 1. https://www.fda.gov/food/outbreaks -foodborne-illness/fda-investigation-cronobacter-infections-powdered-infant -formula-february-2022.

Jung, Jinho, Nicole Olynk Widmar, and Brenna Ellison. 2022. "The Curious Case of Baby Formula in the United States in 2022: Cries for Urgent Action Months After Silence in the Midst of Alarm Bells." *Food Ethics.* https://link.springer .com/article/10.1007/s41055-022-00115-1.

Widmar, Nicole Olynk, and Courtney Bir. 2022. "Questioning the Value of 'Thoughts and Prayers' for Natural Disaster Victims." *Consumer Corner.* April 4. https://agribusiness.purdue.edu/consumer_corner/questioning-the-value-of -thoughts-and-prayers-for-natural-disaster-victims/.

Adapted from original posting as *ConsumerCorner.2022.Letter.47* (https://agribusiness.purdue.edu/consumer_corner/baby-formula/)

16

GRAPPLING WITH EVOLVING CONSUMER DEMANDS FOR ENVIRONMENTAL ATTRIBUTES

T he rise of social media has created an environment of flash publicity. Products and companies become glorified or vilified faster than we can remember to check our email. Producers, even those buried deep in the value chain, can now become overnight internet sensations for good and bad reasons. Even if online sentiment has not yet crossed your mind, perhaps it should now!

We examined consumer sentiment from 2018 to 2021 on livestock products and their carbon emissions. These conversations came in the wake of a century of agricultural intensification and productivity growth, trends that, in some ways, have coincided with improved environmental performance on farms. Farmers have also become increasingly exposed to carbon markets.

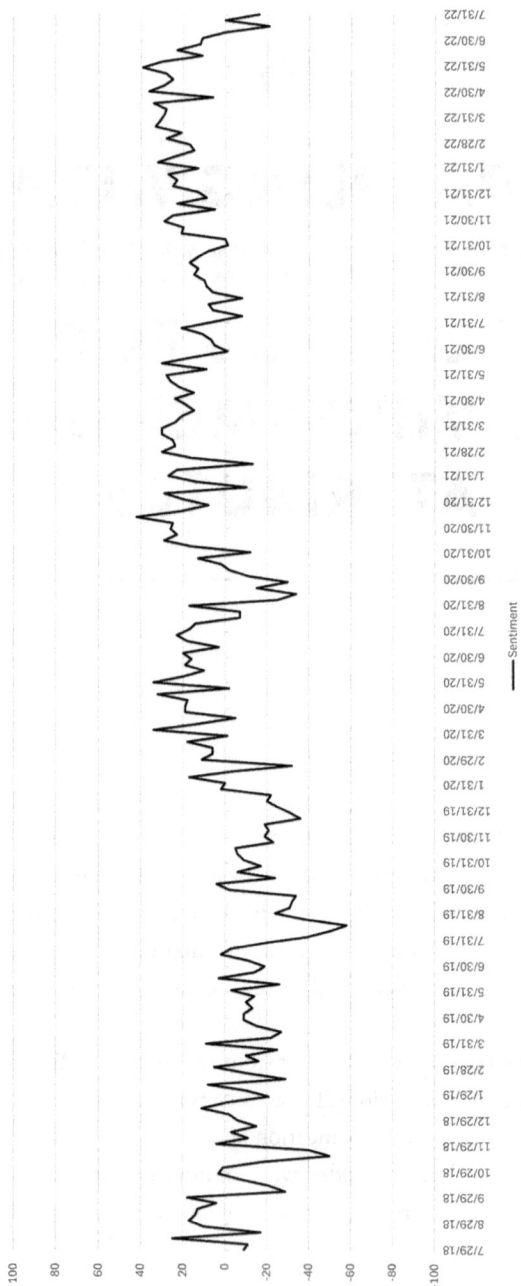

FIGURE 16.1. Net Sentiment of Carbon in Online Media, 2018–2022

While some activists push for more rapid progress, we reiterate a common finding on *Consumer Corner*. The consumer does not always know what they want. Remember 2019? A wave of scorn for single-use plastic swept the nation, and retailers including Starbucks moved quickly to eliminate straws and promote reusable cups. But as fast as the reusable cups integrated, they were removed for public health concerns as the pandemic began. In fact, the way consumers behaved under duress reminds us we must remain agile in our marketing, messaging, and product placement (Book One, chapter 2). Just as reusable cup advocacy vanished from retail stores, discussions about environmental consequences also faded from online platforms. As shown in Figure 16.1, we can see that during the COVID-19 lockdown period (March 2020–June 2021), sentiment scores in online media trended mostly positive.

But what goes around comes around. As producers, we ought to recall that markets can change on a dime, and consumer sentiment can too. Just as concerns about the health of the meat supply chain arose and subsided quickly (Book Three, chapter 14), we saw public interest migrating to a more positive discussion of the environment, focused on solutions as opposed to world-ending tragedies. We find that consumers are now interested in what companies are doing to practice sustainability, and they love family farms! Agribusinesses would be wise to respond to this call, but wiser still to avoid being "all hat and no cattle."

———————————

Adapted from original posting as *ConsumerCorner.2023.Letter.14* (https://agribusiness.purdue.edu/consumer_corner/grappling-with -evolving-consumer-demands-for-environmental-attributes/)

17

DO YOU ENJOY YOUR "FALL BACK" TO STANDARD TIME?

D o you ever wonder about daylight saving time? We do.

We all hear a lot of talk about daylight saving time, but it seems to happen mostly around the time jumps themselves. Ask yourself, how often do you talk about it in the middle of July? This change is exalted by some for blessing us with an extra hour of sleep in the fall (when clocks "fall back" an hour) and condemned by others for its cruel "spring forward" of time in the spring. However, those of us blessed with children, dogs, and cats (among other companions you may enlist) are reminded that this clever clock-play is merely a human construct. Whether it is our kids waking up, or our pets and livestock wanting to be fed, our circadian rhythms do not yield to adjustments of the clock. If you happen to belong to the group unable to enjoy or deride the ritual, don't bother trying to remember your thoughts on it before adopting your current lifestyle—it can be tough to remember.

As the seasons change, so might our preferences. After all, who doesn't like extra sleep? And who wouldn't complain about being robbed of the hour we borrowed a few months prior? In the end, who likes change,

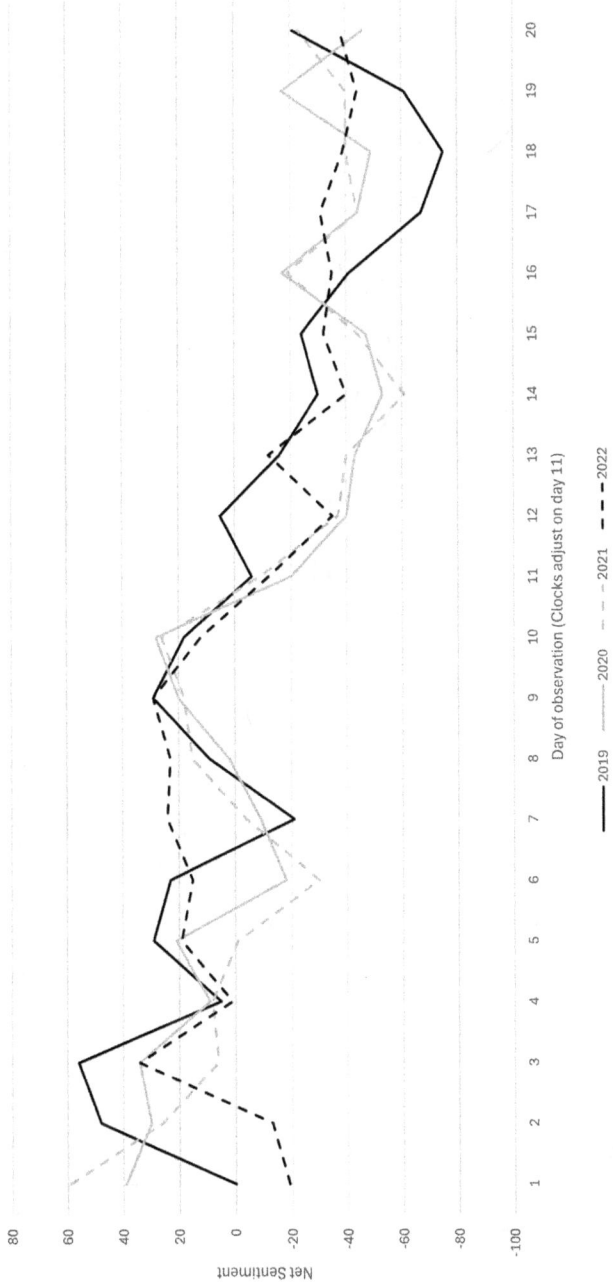

FIGURE 17.1. Net Sentiment, by Year, When Clocks "Fall Back"

Day of observation (Clocks adjust on day 11)

2019 —— 2020 — — 2021 — — 2022

Net Sentiment

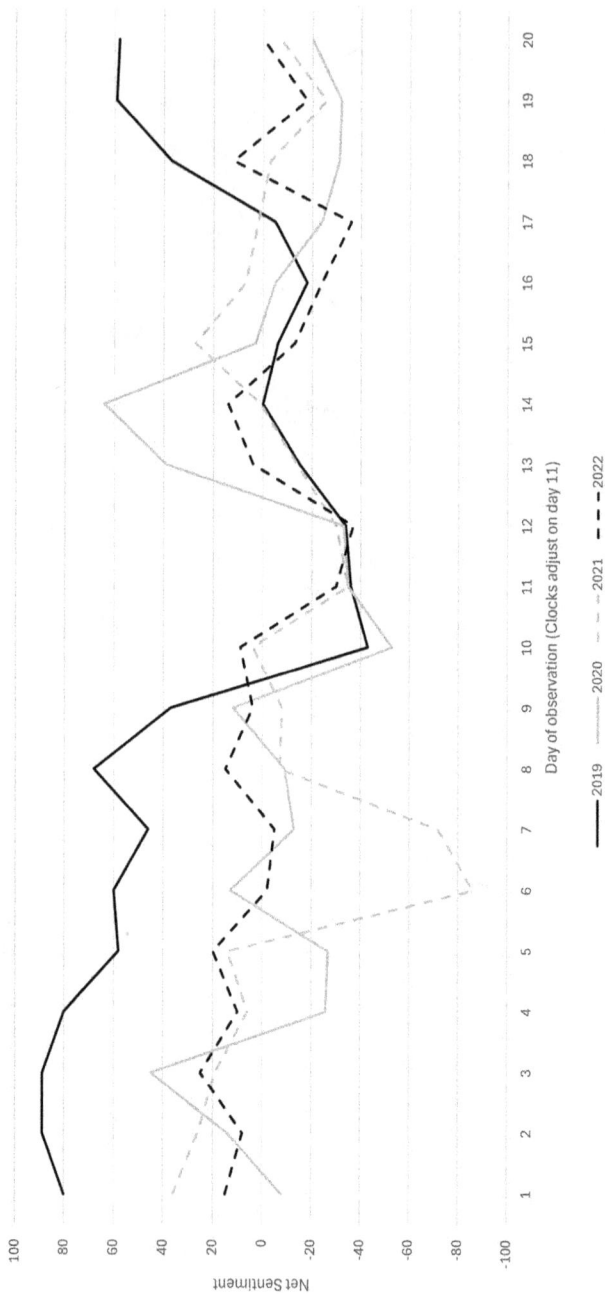

FIGURE 17.2. Net Sentiment, by Year, When Clocks "Spring Forward"

anyway? If the changing of the clocks irks us both in the fall and again in the spring, what are we even doing here?

Lucky for us social scientists, the internet is full of our opinions on the matter, and there is no shortage of complaints. In fact, the US Congress regularly debates the issue, so far without resolution. All of this begs the question: Who cares? And about what exactly? And does it even matter?

Well, rest assured; it *does* matter. Time is money, after all. Through the power of web scraping, we were able to discern the opinions of those of us brave enough to post our thoughts online. Below, we graph average sentiment from ten days before and ten days after each of the clock-jumping events in the past four years. Sentiment scores are determined using natural language processing of social media, news media, and blog posts within the United States.

In fall, when we get an extra hour of sleep, we see some excitement (positive sentiment) beforehand, only for it to give way to negativity when it actually occurs.

In spring, we see a similar (albeit noisier) trend. Excusing the dubious optimism of 2020—when we were likely depressed about other things— the idea of something "normal" to be upset about, like the time change, was potentially relatively comforting.

We do see an overall higher average sentiment leading into daylight saving time when we fall back, compared to springtime when we spring forward. However, even the positive sentiment is not overwhelming, and we note a slightly negative outlook on the whole thing overall. Perhaps an ode to our love of routine? Maybe reflective of just how much we dislike change? It never seems to be a positive thing, and we're routinely debating the merits versus costs. Ongoing research will seek to understand *why* we continue to do it, and whether opinions vary by geographic location.

Adapted from original posting as *ConsumerCorner.2023.Letter.28* (https://www.agribusiness.purdue.edu/consumer_corner/did-you-enjoy -your-fall-back-to-standard-time/)

18

THE GOOGLE SEARCH BAR KNOWS A LOT ABOUT YOU (AND ME, AND EVERYONE!)

O nline and social media data are a new frontier of information. But social media has its (many) challenges. You post only your best life on Twitter and Facebook. You might say that the curated feed that results is not accurate, and not everyone is well represented. It's likely true, but who are we to say? As the content creator of your own online self, *you* designed it, not us.

Yet, there is another online data source that knows more about us than social media could ever hope to. It isn't curated for others to see—in fact, it's often the stuff that nobody else will ever see or hear from you. And that's precisely why you turn to it. It's that little text bar into which we type our deepest secrets, even the really, *really* unflattering stuff—the kind that would (and should) make other people recoil: the Google search bar and the data it generates.

Seth Stephens-Davidowitz's book *Everybody Lies: Big Data, New Data, and What the Internet Can Tell Us About Who We Really Are* discusses this concept using Google search data. People tell Google things they might not tell anyone else: not their friends, their spouse, or their doctor (Stephens-Davidowitz 2017). Considering how much better Google search data reflects reality in the topics explored in the book compared to survey data or other more traditional data sources, it seems that we're not as prone to lying to Google (or at least not nearly as much).

Let's face it: The Black Friday mayhem isn't exactly a flattering look for society. The day before, we give thanks for all we have as we watch the news to see people fighting one another (and not just figuratively) for a reduced-price small kitchen appliance.

We gathered 7,043,573 online and social media posts about shopping during the Thanksgiving weekend through Cyber Monday (Widmar 2023). Overall, Cyber Monday generated far fewer posts and mentions but with a higher net sentiment. Given that Black Friday shoppers often wait in lines in the cold, face altercations with over-eager fellow shoppers, and engage in a physical hunt for products (which might sell out before they get to them), it's not hard to imagine the associated negatives. Cyber Monday, in contrast, can be undertaken in your pajamas from the comfort of your smartphone. Thus, the higher net sentiment is believable and reasonable.

Given the nature of social media data and the availability of Google Search data on the topic, we sought to investigate whether online searches about shopping, Black Friday, and Cyber Monday mirrored the timing associated with the growth in conversations on social media. Google Search data is presented as "interest over time" rather than absolute numbers of media posts or mentions. Specifically: "Numbers represent search interest relative to the highest point on the chart for the given region and time. A value of 100 is the peak popularity for the term. A value of 50 means that the term is half as popular. A score of 0 means there was not enough data for this term."

The analysis spans five years of web search data focusing on shopping, Black Friday, and Cyber Monday. It's worth noting that the peak popularity for both "shopping" and "Black Friday" occurred during the week of November 24, 2019. As anticipated, "Cyber Monday" peaked in popularity one week later, during the week of December 1, 2019. One other

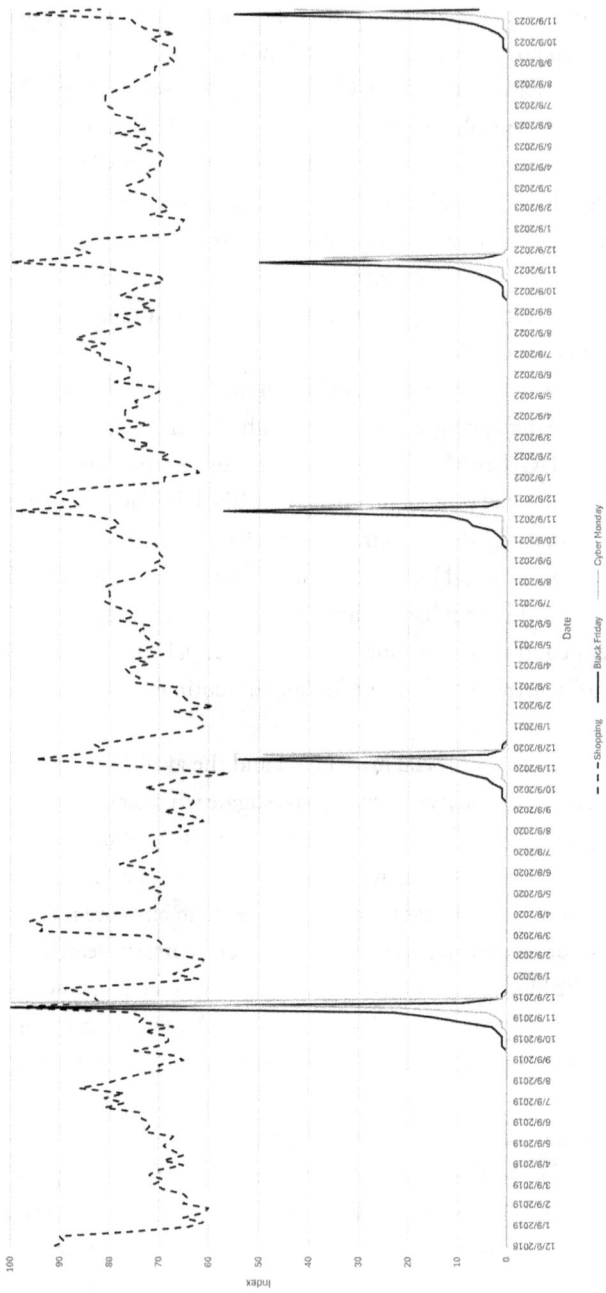

FIGURE 18.1. Five Years of Google Web Search Trends on Shopping, Black Friday, and Cyber Monday

peak in shopping searched occurred during the week of November 20, 2022. Interestingly, overall interest in shopping never dropped below 56. Predictably, Black Friday and Cyber Monday predominantly register at 0, with pronounced but short-lived spikes in searches during consecutive weeks each year.

In this case, examining shopping with a focus on the post-Thanksgiving holiday period shows that both online/social media data and Google Search data reflect real-world interest in the topic. In other words, these digital traces mirror reality as measured in retail spending, going-to-market activity, and the like. Even though adults physically fighting over a toy in a retail establishment is unflattering, it seems we're rather consistent in what we search for versus what we talk about. Of course, numerous other topics exist where search data and social media data may not align—particularly topics that are more sensitive in nature, perhaps, or even less flattering than instances of retail aggression.

WORKS CITED

Stephens-Davidowitz, Seth. 2017. *Everybody Lies: Big Data, New Data, and What the Internet Can Tell Us About Who We Really Are.* Dey Street Books.

Widmar, Nicole J. Olynk. 2023. "Unspoken Records of Cyber Monday Amid Black Friday Buzz." November 28. https://agribusiness.purdue.edu/consumer_corner /unspoken-records-of-cyber-monday-amid-black-friday-buzz/.

Adapted from original posting as *ConsumerCorner.2023.Letter.30* (https://agribusiness.purdue.edu/consumer_corner/the-google-search -bar-knows-a-lot-about-you-and-me-and-everyone/)

19

UNSPOKEN RECORDS OF CYBER MONDAY AMID BLACK FRIDAY BUZZ

<hr>

Thanksgiving is a time for giving thanks, time with family, and the eve of a uniquely American consumer: Black Friday shoppers. Retailers use Black Friday for marketing, but few people likely recognize why it's called that. The *Wall Street Journal* summarized this cultural phenomenon (Pisani 2023). Black Friday is when retailers enter "the black," leaving "the red," and start generating profits for the year. Other days with "black" in their name are generally bad, like Black Monday for stock market crashes. There were attempts to rebrand Black Friday over the years, but nothing stuck and Black Friday remains today.

Investopedia reported that Black Friday online spending reached a record high in 2023 ($9.8 billion), which is up 7.5 percent from the previous year (Attarwala 2023). CNN reported that Americans were set to spend a record $12 billion in online shopping on Cyber Monday (Egan 2023). That's after Black Friday sales were already known to be very strong, especially Black Friday spending online. This is all happening amid continued concerns around inflation and higher interest rates impacting households' finances.

We already know from multiple years of inquiry in the past that Friendsgiving has a higher associated sentiment than Thanksgiving (Widmar and Bir 2020). That finding was hard for many people to receive, but consider the definitions of these celebrations. For many people (not necessarily you—don't worry), Friendsgiving *feels* better. It's evident in how we talk about it.

According to Merriam-Webster (2025b), Thanksgiving is "a day appointed for giving thanks for divine goodness." The legal holiday in the United States was formally appointed to the fourth Thursday of November in 1941, although the origins of the US celebration and feast date back to 1621 (Merriam-Webster 2025b).

In contrast, Friendsgiving appears on Merriam-Webster's "Words We're Watching" list as a way to "escape your family and celebrate with friends." The dictionary notes the earliest print mention of the word is in 2007, although admits it floated around in spoken English before then. Contrary to what many people think, Friendsgiving did not originate on the TV show *Friends*. The term rose to prominence in 2011 when Baileys Irish Cream used it in an ad campaign (Merriam-Webster (2025a).

After years of wrestling with the data to settle the Thanksgiving versus Friendsgiving debate (and finding the same clear winner every time), I've decided to tackle a different argument: Black Friday versus Cyber Monday. We adapted our holiday celebrations during the pandemic (Widmar 2021), and while I don't have the specific data to speak to it, I suspect that the adaptation of holiday shopping also took place. We know that the adoption of online shopping was well underway (and so was Cyber Monday!) before 2020. Yet, I presume the fear of being in crowded stores pushed us even further along this path toward seeking online deals, in addition to or in place of brick-and-mortar store deals during the winter holiday shopping season.

Using Quid, which we have relied on to gather data for analysis for a variety of topics of public interest, we examined online conversations about shopping over the 2023 holiday weekend. As the saying goes, time is money, and seasons—and preferences—change (see Book Two, chapter 19).

We gathered online media mentions of at least one of the terms from our list: shop, shopping, Cyber Monday, Black Friday, CyberMonday, BlackFriday, #BlackFriday, and #CyberMonday from November 1, 2023, to the end of November 2023. There were 7,043,573 posts in total, of which the vast majority (76 percent, totaling over 5.3 million) came from Twitter/X. The overall net sentiment was 64 percent on the scale of possible net sentiment, which ranges from -100 percent to +100 percent.

Of these posts, 16.6 percent were from news media posts, many of which focused on business trends and holiday spending projections. There were also reviews, especially product reviews, on various sites, blogs, and platforms. The vast majority of the posts and mentions happened after November 19. Online media content that matched the keywords we specified exhibits a positive sentiment. Among the total results, we saw a +64 percent net sentiment. But when we narrowed our focus to the three terms that directly reference Black Friday, the net sentiment rose to +69 percent amid the 2,715,047 mentions.

There were far fewer direct mentions of the three Cyber Monday terms. In total, we saw 482,281 mentions from November 1, but with a higher net sentiment of 84 percent. The volume of mentions about Cyber Monday peaked later than Black Friday, largely amassing over the weekend following Thanksgiving, rather than in anticipation of it.

Many of the top terms overlapped when people were talking about these two shopping events—best, amazing, and sale, for example. The top five terms in the search results, in order, for Cyber Monday were deals, sale, out, save, and Cyber Monday Deal. The top five for Black Friday were deals, sale, Black Friday deals, Black Friday Sales, and #blackfriday.

Overall, Cyber Monday saw fewer total mentions, but with higher net sentiment. That makes intuitive sense. Black Friday often involves long lines in the cold weather and the occasional altercation with a fellow shopper—all in pursuit of a product that might sell out before you get to it. Cyber Monday, in contrast, can be enjoyed from the comfort of one's pajamas via smartphone. The higher net sentiment is believable and reasonable. As for the lower volume of discussion, it may reflect a broader trend: Perhaps online shopping events simply generate fewer shareable moments. When purchases are made with a few quick taps rather than long lines or chaotic crowds, there's less drama—and less to talk about. We scroll, we click, we buy, and it's done. Without parking lot standoffs or sidewalk campouts, the experience becomes more routine than remarkable. It's possible this shift in behavior contributes to a quieter digital footprint. Whether that trend continues remains to be seen.

WORKS CITED

Attarwala, F. (2023 , November 27). *US Cyber Monday Sales Online Could Top $12B After Record Black Friday, Adobe Says*. Retrieved from *investopedia.com*: https://www.investopedia.com/us-cyber-monday-sales-online-could-top-usd12b-after-record-black-friday-adobe-says-8406715

Egan, M. (2023, November 27). *Americans Are Set to Spend a Record $12 Billion Online Shopping Today*. Retrieved from *cnn.com/2023*: https://www.cnn.com/2023/11/27/business/record-setting-holiday-sales/index.html

Merriam-Webster. (2025a, July 3). *Friendsgiving*. Retrieved from *merriam-webster.com/dictionary*: https://www.merriam-webster.com/dictionary/Friendsgiving

Merriam-Webster. (2025b, July 3). *Thanksgiving Day*. Retrieved from *merriam-webster.com/dictionary*: https://www.merriam-webster.com/dictionary/Thanksgiving%20Day

Pisani, J. (2023, November 24). *Decades of Black Friday Deals: A History of America's Favorite Shopping Day*. Retrieved from *wsj.com/story*: https://www.wsj.com/story/decades-of-black-friday-deals-a-history-of-americas-favorite-shopping-day-d471cc3d

Widmar, N. O. (2021, January 4). *2020 Holiday Season Adaptations*. Retrieved from *Consumer Corner*: https://agribusiness.purdue.edu/consumer_corner/2020-holiday-season-adaptations/.

Widmar, N. O., & Bir, C. (2020, November 3). *Friendsgiving: The Holiday That (Historically) Kept on Giving—2020 Investigation*. Retrieved from *Consumer Corner*: https://agribusiness.purdue.edu/consumer_corner/friendsgiving-2020-investigation/.

Adapted from original posting as *ConsumerCorner.2023.Letter.29* (https://agribusiness.purdue.edu/consumer_corner/unspoken-records-of-cyber-monday-amid-black-friday-buzz/)

20

LIMITED EDITION AND SEASONAL FOOD

BY NICOLE J. OLYNK WIDMAR AND VALERIE KILDERS
with special thanks to the #Data research team in the
Department of Agricultural Economics at Purdue University,
including Michael L. Smith, Zachary Neuhofer,
Sachina Kagaya, and Austin Berenda

T is the season to be overindulgent, it seems—and it's not just food we're indulging in. We used social and online media data to explore the buzz around holiday shopping during the Thanksgiving holiday weekend. Then, in the last chapter, we looked at Google Search data about Black Friday, Cyber Monday, and shopping overall. But reliably, we always come back to food in our conversations—something the data visibly seems to support, particularly when it comes to seasonal or limited-edition food items.

I'm not sure if we've just been incredibly well conditioned or if we all just really feel the need to search for Pumpkin Spice in October each year due to deeply seated biological drives. Consumers are constantly claiming to be heterogeneous with varying tastes and preferences. It's true, after all. We have heterogeneous tastes and preferences. But we get awfully homogenous, it seems, when we're all seemingly kicking off Peppermint Mocha season on practically the same day every year!

We're back working with our little search bar on the screen that knows our deepest, darkest, and sometimes weirdest secrets: the Google Search bar and its data. Knowing what people are searching for and talking about can be helpful in understanding ever-evolving consumer demands. In this case, it can help us understand consumers' timeline in following their inherent desire to add some seasonal flavors and colors to their drink or add fast-food cult classics to their diet.

We'll remind you that Google Search data is presented as "interest over time." Specifically, "Numbers represent search interest relative to the highest point on the chart for the given region and time. A value of 100 is the peak popularity for the term. A value of 50 means that the term is half as popular. A score of 0 means there was not enough data for this term."

We looked at Google Search data for Pumpkin Spice, Peppermint Mocha, Shamrock Shake, and the McRib. Admittedly, these are three intentionally seasonal items, plus the McRib. The McRib is limited edition, but not seasonal per se. The official wording is, "But its availability is limited—we'll make sure to let you know when the McRib is back" (McDonalds, 2025). Yet, it seems to return each year in November (Lamour, 2023). When the McRib returns, so does interest in searching for it, as evidenced by Google search activity.

We are incredibly consistent in our seasonal food quests. Not only do we search for these items consistently, but our interest also spikes and fades in predictable patterns. For example, search interest in Pumpkin Spice builds early in the fall and declines gradually—though it remains high well into Peppermint Mocha season. Similarly, Peppermint Mocha searches come out strong, peak early, and taper off through the New Year. The Shamrock Shake, however, follows a different path: It tends to rise slowly in interest and peaks later in its brief seasonal window.

It's December, a time for holiday cheer and shopping. More specifically, it's December 12, which for five years in a row marks the precise time that interest in the Peppermint Mocha, as measured by Google web search data, is on the decline from its recent peak. That's not just a flippant remark. Consumers are so unbelievably consistent in their interest in the Peppermint Mocha that we felt the need to bring forward the raw data. We present Peppermint Mocha interest in 2021, which peaks the week of November 7 and then heads downward. December 12 is highlighted for

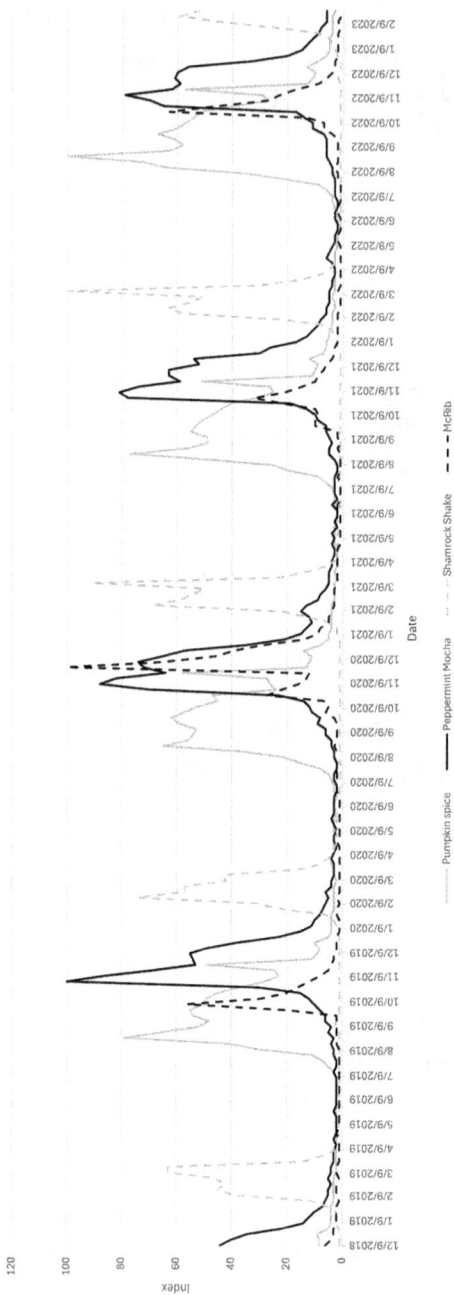

FIGURE 20.1. Interest in Seasonal Food Items Measured Using Google Search Data

TABLE 20.1. *Interest in the Peppermint Mocha Over Time*

MOCHA SEASON 2021	INTEREST IN PEPPERMINT MOCHA	MOCHA SEASON 2022	INTEREST IN PEPPERMINT MOCHA
10/3/2021	8	10/2/2022	9
10/10/2021	11	10/9/2022	10
10/17/2021	15	10/16/2022	15
10/24/2021	19	10/23/2022	19
10/31/2021	78	10/30/2022	62
11/7/2021	88	11/6/2022	68
11/14/2021	72	11/13/2022	78
11/21/2021	64	11/20/2022	61
11/28/2021	66	11/27/2022	60
12/5/2021	62	12/4/2022	60
12/12/2021	53	12/11/2022	58
12/19/2021	51	12/18/2022	58
12/26/2021	30	12/25/2022	33
1/2/2022	26	1/1/2023	21
1/9/2022	16	1/8/2023	16
1/16/2022	14	1/15/2023	14
1/23/2022	11	1/22/2023	11
1/30/2022	8	1/29/2023	9
2/6/2022	8	2/5/2023	8
2/13/2022	6	2/12/2023	6
2/20/2022	6	2/19/2023	7
2/27/2022	5	2/26/2023	6

ease; interest was 53. Not convinced? Let's look at 2022. Interest peaks the week of November 13 and then declines. The week of December 11, interest came in at 58.

We're embarrassingly consistent. I mean, are we really that predictable? Short answer = yes. We took a close look at the nuances of 2022 and 2023, but there are none. While preferences are heterogeneous among individual consumers, it turns out we, as a nation, are remarkably conditioned for seasonal fast-food items. Or there's an instinctive, biological craving for the Shamrock Shake and Peppermint Mocha at the exact same times each year, following the same pattern of interest. I suppose that could be true (although it's not).

WORKS CITED

Lamour, J. (2023). *McDonald's McRib Returns*. Retrieved from *today.com /food/restaurants*: https://www.today.com/food/restaurants/mcdonalds-mcrib -return-2023-rcna118129.

McDonalds. (2025). *McRib*. Retrieved from *mcdonalds.com/us/en-us/product*: https://www.mcdonalds.com/us/en-us/product/mcrib.html.

Adapted from original posting as *ConsumerCorner.2023.Letter.31* (https://www.agribusiness.purdue.edu/consumer_corner/limited-edition -and-seasonal-food/)

21

NEW DRINKS ARE ALL THE RAGE, BUT THEY AREN'T AS BOOZY ANYMORE

February might be the shortest month of the year, but it contains two notable dates that are culturally linked to indulgence (and potentially overindulgence) of alcoholic beverages: Superbowl Sunday and Valentine's Day. Often, events like these are celebrated with some sort of festivity, usually including the (responsible) consumption of alcoholic beverages. Furthermore, references to holidays and related celebrations are common in online and social media data.

The alcohol industry in the United States holds significant social and economic influence, with a long-standing presence in advertising and holiday celebrations, and many Americans report drinking alcohol on a weekly basis (Gallup 2024). Surveys of alcohol use in the United States since the 1970s have consistently found that roughly 60 percent of adults consume alcoholic beverages. However, breaking this down by age shows us that the rate of 18- to 34-year-olds drinking has fallen around 10 percent since the early 2000s (from 72 percent to 62 percent), while drinking among adults 55 and older has increased from 49 percent to 59 percent (Gallup 2023).

Some of the declines in drinking alcoholic beverages have been offset by an increase in consumption of specifically nonalcoholic drink offerings, such as nonalcoholic beer and mocktails (McLymore 2025). These mocktails and related nonalcoholic drinks may have strong flavor profiles, which increasingly appeal to consumers (Rawat 2023). The medical community is strengthening its long-held view that alcohol use negatively affects the human body, recently declaring that no level of alcohol consumption is safe for human health (WHO 2023). Conclusions of the effect of alcohol on human health are backed by decades of evidence-based research (MacMahon 1987; Bujanda 2000; Eckardt et al. 2006; Rehm 2011; Becker 2012; WHO 2023).

Consumers choice has expanded. Choice surveys find that increasing availability of healthier options leads to increased consumption of those options, which is true for both food and beverages. Online, this pattern holds for nonalcoholic beverages. When consumers are presented with both alcoholic and nonalcoholic beverages, many opt for the latter (Blackwell et al. 2020). While alcohol purchasing online might not be the norm, shopping for groceries online is increasingly popular. A similar study of online shoppers corroborates this (Clarke et al. 2023). Additionally, we know that Americans have long exhibited a slight preference for beer compared to liquor or wine (Gallup 2024).

Purdue University researchers wondered if we could see these trends emerge in online media data generated by news and social media posts. Social media data has been useful for us to study public perceptions of Daylight Saving Time, #Halloween, and #Galentine's day, so why not alcoholic beverages? We analyzed social media mentions of five beverage categories—beer, wine, spirits, seltzers, and nonalcoholic drinks—from March 1, 2023 to June 1, 2024. Additionally, we measured net sentiment, which is a useful metric derived by analyzing some of these mentions in a natural language processor, assigning the mentions a positive, negative, or neutral sentiment based on context and tone. We take a weekly ratio of positive to negative mentions and report a net sentiment score. Looking at numbers of mentions and the associated sentiment of search results over time can show how preferences might change according to the time of year. After all, seasons change and so do consumption patterns; might media discussions about beverages follow suit?

Trends in the data show mentions of beer, spirits, and seltzers fall throughout the collection period, but we see a rise in the number of weekly mentions of wine and nonalcoholic drinks. While weekly net sentiment is mostly positive (indicating more positive mentions than negative mentions about the beverage categories), we see one large blip of negative sentiment in seltzers the week of December 24, 2024, the week of Christmas and Boxing Day. Notice that harsh dip in sentiment corresponds to a large rise in mentions of seltzers. Anecdotally, we tend to notice spikes in mentions are often accompanied by spikes in negative sentiment. From prior experience, we suspect that this could be influenced by having a relatively small sample (when compared to the larger categories).

Because mentions of nonalcoholic and seltzer beverages are relatively low, we put them on their own graph.

We also plot the net sentiment for each beverage category. Note that the graph is messy! We observe very similar (positive) net sentiment scores across categories, indicating that there are more positive posts than negative posts regarding the beverage categories we study.

This all begs the question: What drives the trends we see? A plausible hypothesis would be that online discussion of alcoholic beverages might have seasonal relationships, or perhaps these discussions are driven by holidays. To get to the bottom of this, we computed a simple linear regression of each data series as the dependent variable to be predicted by a dummy variable for federal holidays in the United States. The nature of a dummy variable is such that it takes a binary value (either 0 or 1). In this case the holiday variable = 1 in the week of a federal holiday, and 0 otherwise.

We find that the presence of a federal holiday does not explain the volume of mentions or the net sentiment of these beverages in any case, except for liquor mentions (at the 10 percent significance level) and nonalcoholic drink mentions (at the 1 percent significance level). According to the r^2 statistic, the federal holidays account for 5.5 percent of the variation in liquor mentions and 17.5% of the variation in nonalcoholic beverage mentions. This suggests a relationship between federal holidays and discussions of liquor and nonalcoholic beverages.

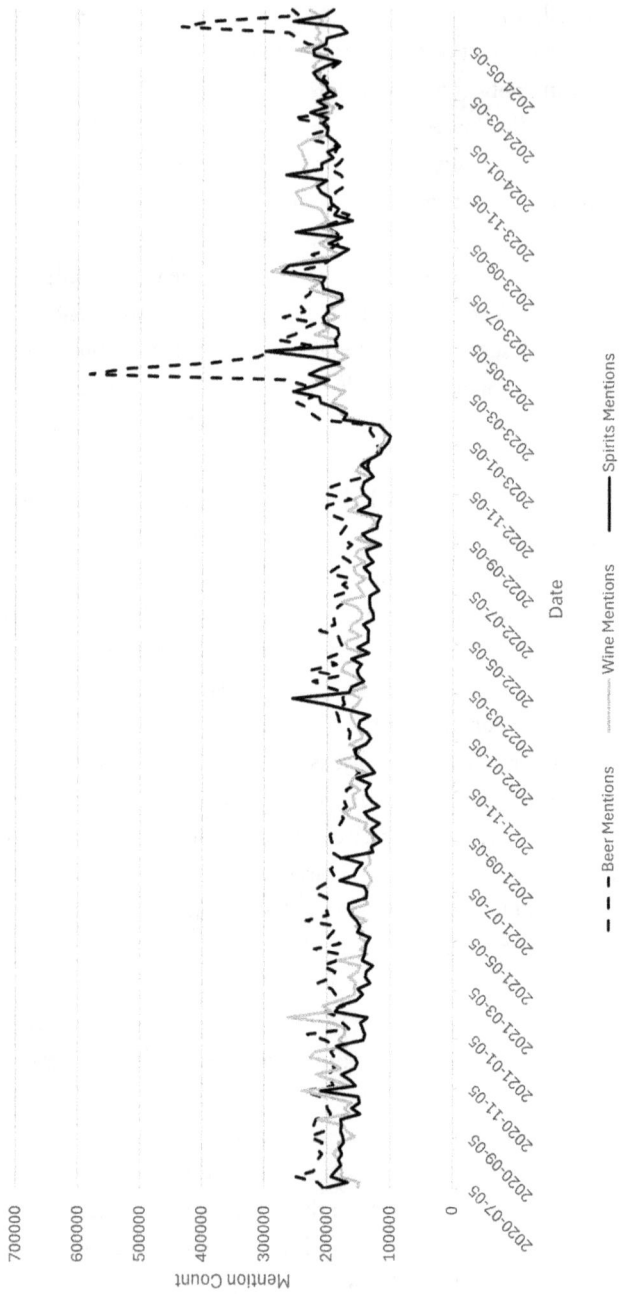

FIGURE 21.1. Mentions of Beer, Spirits, and Wine

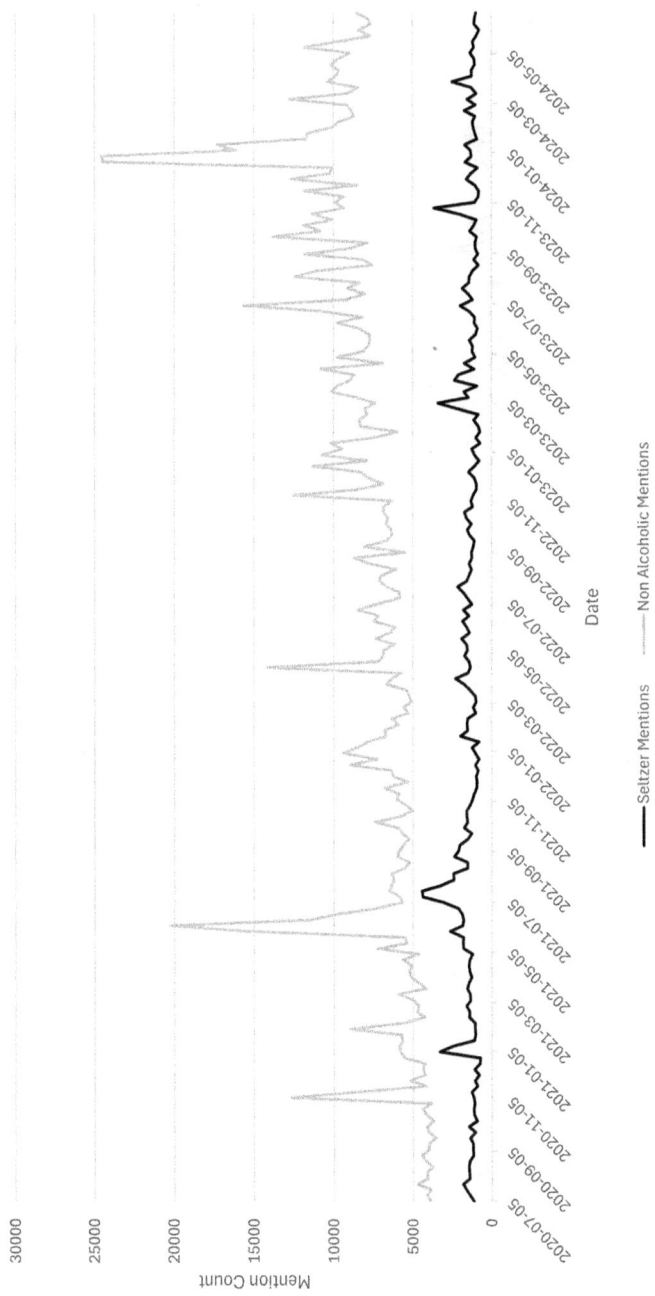

FIGURE 21.2. Mentions of Seltzer and Nonalcoholic Beverages

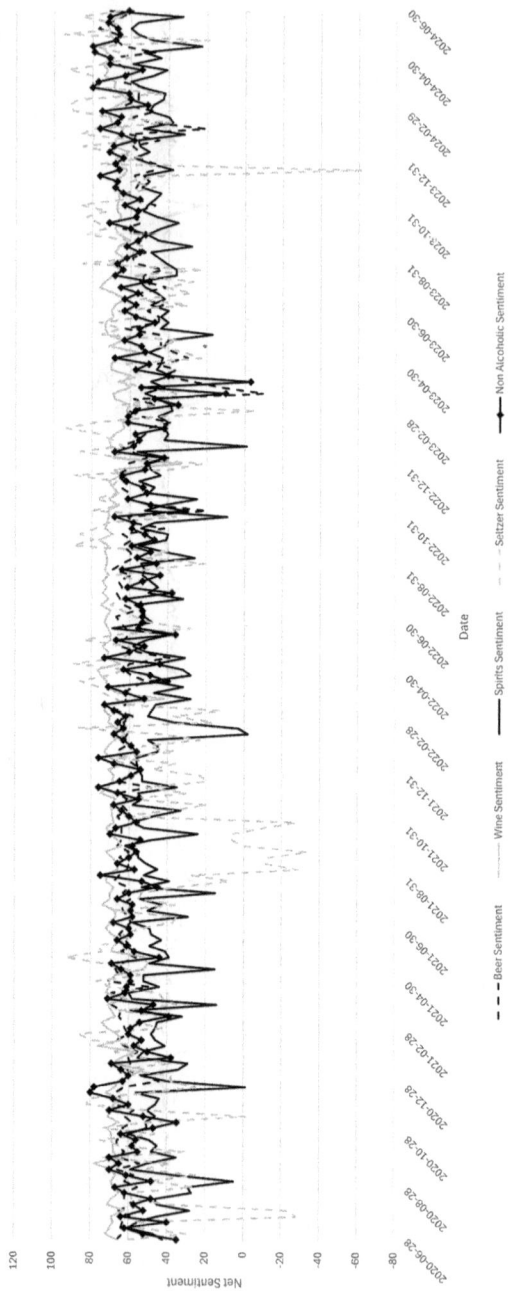

FIGURE 21.3. Net Sentiment of Selected Beverage Categories

Interestingly, when examining the model coefficients, we find that in both cases of liquor and nonalcoholic beverages, the presence of a federal holiday had a negative effect on conversation levels. This is not what we expected. While we expected to find a statistically significant relationship in some categories, we did not expect holidays to have a negative effect on mentions. In fact, we would have hypothesized the opposite. There is no case in which the presence of a federal holiday explains the net sentiment of a beverage category.

While there is a profitable and very real intersection between the agriculture and adult beverage industries, that is not the point of this Consumer Corner entry. Our point is that industries outside of beverages can learn valuable lessons from how this sector adapts. The beverage industry has found a way to meet the needs of consumers who are more conscious of their health, selective about the flavors they consume, and increasingly motivated to look for local suppliers with strong environmental attributes—trends that extend beyond alcohol. These are big themes we see along agricultural value chains as well. Just as nonalcoholic beverages and seltzers have given producers new ways to cater to diverse consumer preferences, other industries will need to capitalize on their own market disrupters. Without a doubt, the beverage industry needs big-data solutions to understand its changing, multifaceted consumers. And without a doubt, your industry can benefit too.

WORKS CITED

Becker, Howard. 2012. "Effects of Alcohol Dependence and Withdrawal on Stress Responsiveness and Alcohol Consumption." *Alcohol Research* 448–458.

Blackwell, Anna, Katie De-loyde, Gareth Hollands, Richard Morris, Laura Brocklebank, Olivia Maynard, Paul Fletcher, Theresa Marteau, and Marcus Munafo. 2020. "The Impact on Selection of Non-Alcoholic vs Alcoholic Drink Availability: An Online Experiment." *BMC Public Health.* https://bmcpublichealth .biomedcentral.com/articles/10.1186/s12889-020-08633-5.

Bujanda, Luis. 2000. "The Effects of Alcohol Consumption Upon the Gastrointestinal Tract." *American Journal of Gastroenterology* 3374–3382.

Clarke, Natasha, Anna Blackwell, Jennifer Ferrar, Katie De-Loyde, Mark Pilling, Marcus Munafo, Theresa Marteau, and Gareth Hollands. 2023. "Impact on Alcohol Selection and Online Purchasing of Changing the Proportion of Available Non-Alcoholic Versus Alcoholic Drinks: A Randomised Controlled Trial." *pubmed.ncbi.nlm.nih.gov.*

Eckardt, Michael J., Sandra E. File, Gian Luigi Gessa, Kathleen A. Grant, Consuelo Guerri, Paula L. Hoffman, Harold Kalant, George F. Koob, Ting-Kai Li, and Boris Tabakoff. 2006. "Effects of Moderate Alcohol Consumption on the Central Nervous System." *Alcoholism: Clinical and Experimental Research* 998–1040.

Gallup. 2023. "Young Adults in U.S. Drinking Less Than in Prior Decades." August 22. https://news.gallup.com/poll/509690/young-adults-drinking-less-prior-decades.aspx#:~:text=Young%20Adults%20Now%20Vie%20With ,from%2049%25%20to%2059%25.

Gallup. 2024. "Alcohol and Drinking." *news.gallup.com.* https://news.gallup.com/poll/1582/alcohol-drinking.aspx.

MacMahon, Stephen. 1987. "Alcohol Consumption and Hypertension." *Hypertension: American Health Association.*

McLymore, Arriana. 2025. "Even Before US Alcohol Warning, Younger Americans Were Turning to Mocktails." *Reuters.* January 4th. https://www.reuters.com/world/us/even-before-us-alcohol-warning-younger-americans-were-turning-mocktails-2025-01-04/.

Rawat, A. 2023. "How Consumer Preferences Are Reshaping the Beer Industry." *Brewer World*: https://www.brewer-world.com/how-consumer-preferences-are-reshaping-the-beer-industry/.

Rehm, Jurgen. 2011. "The Risks Associated With Alcohol Use and Alcoholism." *Alcohol Res Health* 135–143.

WHO. 2023. "No Level of Alcohol Consumption Is Safe for Our Health." January 4. https://www.who.int/europe/news/item/04-01-2023-no-level-of-alcohol-consumption-is-safe-for-our-health.

Adapted from original posting as *ConsumerCorner.2025.Letter.03* (https://agribusiness.purdue.edu/consumer_corner/new-drinks-are-all-the-rage-but-they-arent-as-boozy-anymore/)

CONCLUSION

Market Signals From Online Behavior

W hen it comes to food and agriculture, production systems are diverse and complex, with businesses serving a variety of needs—from transportation to storage, from field to production to processing, from marketing to packaging—and the list goes on. Uncertainty exists in nearly every aspect of food production systems, much of this stemming from future consumer demands. There are countless debates: Which apple variety will be in demand in three, five, or ten years? Which grape is trending now versus a few years ago? Regardless, one aspect is constant in all of these market transactions: people. On both the production and consumption sides, it's people making the calls. And people, well, come with people problems—or let's call them challenges. Add in the sheer number of people, and we get a lot of data. Big data.

Everyone is talking about big data. Nobody really seems to agree on what it means, but we know it is "big" because we keep saying so. We don't know what big means either, but we think it must be bigger than small data. We all know that we want to make decisions with more information rather than less. And we want more data rather than less data. So, bigger *is* better. But it comes with challenges. Even if we possess big data, we need to do something with it. Otherwise, does big data (or any data) have any value at all? Probably not.

We've developed all kinds of tools to understand how people make decisions. We've invested in farm-level data, ranging from inputs used, weather experienced, prices paid, and yield outcomes. There are investments made in understanding how consumers behave when they seek out products in physical stores versus online marketplaces. We want to know what attributes people desire in a product and how those demands vary across consumers with varying demographics, willingness to pay, and shopping occasions. All of these investments in data about human behavior yield data. Sometimes we have measured data in the form of X units of input applied to a specific Y area of ground. Sometimes we have productivity and yield data measured by machinery during harvest. Sometimes we gather it through surveys, interviews, or focus groups—asking people what they want, what they did, what they intend to do, or what they think about X, Y, or Z. And now, of course, there's social media. People telling the whole wide world what they think, want, know (or think they know). It's unpredictable, raw, and sometimes unfiltered—but it's data. A whole new, massive, and messy kind of data.

Perhaps what's more interesting, and central to this volume and the entire *Consumer Corner* series, is not what we can learn about people, but rather what we can learn from them. This edition has featured some of our more colorful and sometimes unsettling corners of the online world. But we're not done. We will keep exploring novel data, evolving data uses, emerging market insights, strategies for building resilience—and, finally, we will be rethinking a lot of what we think we know. After all, consumers are fickle. They're demanding. They're (seemingly) uninformed. They're you.

ABOUT THE AUTHORS

Nicole J. Olynk Widmar is an agricultural economist specializing in farm businesses and consumer decision-making under uncertainty. She serves as a professor and the head of the Department of Agricultural Economics at Purdue University.

Michael L. Smith is a research scientist specializing in the human dimensions of resource use, applying cross-disciplinary methods in agricultural economics and the social sciences. He works in Purdue University's Department of Agricultural Economics.

Erin Robinson is a communications and marketing professional with experience in agricultural business and academic research environments. As marketing manager for Purdue University's Center for Food and Agricultural Business, she develops marketing strategies, creates content and outreach initiatives, drives brand awareness, and evaluates marketing effectiveness.

ABOUT THE CONTRIBUTORS

Courtney Bir is an associate professor of agricultural economics at Oklahoma State University. Her research examines consumer preferences for agricultural products and production economics, aiming to align preferences with profitability. Her extension work focuses on farm finance and operational goal achievement.

Scott Downey is the director of the Center for Food and Agricultural Business and a professor in the Department of Agricultural Economics. He teaches in many of the center's programs, as well as leading sales and marketing courses of over 300 undergraduate students each semester.

Brenna Ellison is a professor of Agribusiness Management and the Undergraduate Programs coordinator in the Department of Agricultural Economics at Purdue University. Her research focuses on how consumers make food choices, including what consumers choose not to eat, or waste.

Aissa Good serves as managing director for the Center for Food and Agricultural Business and the Center for Commercial Agriculture in the Department of Agricultural Economics.

Jinho Jung is a research associate at the Department of Agricultural Economics and Center for Food Demand Analysis and Sustainability of Purdue University. His research interests are in structural/empirical industrial organization, agribusiness, marketing analytics, business strategy, consumer behavior, big data analytics inclusive of social media analytics, and online data scraping in agricultural and food economics.

Valerie Kilders's research leverages food marketing, agribusiness, and experimental economics to understand how consumers and supply chain members make (food) choices and how these decisions affect the food system, agribusinesses, and policies. Her current research agenda focuses on examining responses to scientific advances and evolving consumption patterns to support supply chain stakeholders and inform policy.

John Lai's teaching and research program focuses on agribusiness and marketing. He teaches an online undergraduate course in selling strategically and agricultural marketing strategies, and an online course for graduate students in agribusiness risk management.

Yangxuan Liu focuses on economic issues related to agricultural production and specializes in agricultural finance and agribusiness management. Her research focuses on the economic and risk assessment of existing agricultural systems, as well as emerging technologies and practices, to improve the long-term sustainability and profitability of agricultural production.